The
Seedbed
Daily Text

not receive the things promised; they only saw them and welcomed them from a distance, admitting that they were foreigners and strangers on earth. **People who say such things** show that they are looking for a country of their own. If they had been thinking of the country they had left, they would have had opportunity to return. Instead, they were longing for a better country — a heavenly one. Therefore God is not ashamed to be called their God, for He has prepared a city for them.

Faith

J. D. WALT

Printed in the United States of America

Cover and page design by Strange Last Name
Page layout by PerfecType, Nashville, Tennessee

Walt, John David.
  People who say such things : / J.D. Walt. – Franklin, Tennessee : Seedbed Publishing, ©2020.

pages ; cm. – (Seedbed daily text)

ISBN 9781628248210 (paperback)
ISBN 9781628248227 (Mobi)
ISBN 9781628248234 (ePub)
ISBN 9781628248241 (uPDF)

1. Faith--Meditations. 2. Faith--Biblical teaching.
I. Title. II. Series.

BV4637.W34 2019   234/.23   2020943630

 Seedbed

SEEDBED PUBLISHING
Franklin, Tennessee
seedbed.com

Contents

An Invitation to Awakening

This resource comes with an invitation.

The invitation is as simple as it is comprehensive. It is not an invitation to commit your life to this or that cause or to join an organization or to purchase another book. The invitation is this: to wake up to the life you always hoped was possible and the reason you were put on planet Earth.

It begins with following Jesus Christ. In case you are unaware, Jesus was born in the first century BCE into a poor family from Nazareth, a small village located in what is modern-day Israel. While his birth was associated with extraordinary phenomena, we know little about his childhood. At approximately thirty years of age, Jesus began a public mission of preaching, teaching, and healing throughout the region known as Galilee. His mission was characterized by miraculous signs and wonders; extravagant care of the poor and marginalized; and multiple unconventional claims about his own identity and purpose. In short, he claimed to be the incarnate Son of God with the mission and power to save people from sin, deliver them from death, and bring them into the now-and-eternal kingdom of God—on earth as it is in heaven.

In the spring of his thirty-third year, during the Jewish Passover celebration, Jesus was arrested by the religious authorities, put on trial in the middle of the night, and at their urging, sentenced to death by a Roman governor. On the day known to history as Good Friday, Jesus was crucified on a Roman cross. He was buried in a borrowed tomb. On the following Sunday, according to multiple eyewitness accounts, he was physically raised from the dead. He appeared to hundreds of people, taught his disciples, and prepared for what was to come.

Forty days after the resurrection, Jesus ascended bodily into the heavens where, according to the Bible, he sits at the right hand of God, as the Lord of heaven and earth. Ten days after his ascension, in a gathering of more than three thousand people on the day of Pentecost, a Jewish day of celebration, something truly extraordinary happened. A loud and powerful wind swept over the people gathered. Pillars of what appeared to be fire descended upon the followers of Jesus. The Holy Spirit, the presence and power of God, filled the people, and the church was born. After this, the followers of Jesus went forth and began to do the very things Jesus did—preaching, teaching, and healing—planting churches and making disciples all over the world. Today, more than two thousand years later, the movement has reached us. This is the Great Awakening, and it has never stopped.

Yes, two thousand years and more than two billion followers of Jesus later, this awakening movement of Jesus Christ and his church stands stronger than ever. Billions of ordinary people the world over have discovered in Jesus Christ an awakened life they never imagined possible. They have overcome challenges, defeated addictions, endured untenable hardships and suffering with unexplainable joy, and stared death in the face with the joyful confidence of eternal life. They have healed the sick, gathered the outcasts, embraced the oppressed, loved the poor, contended for justice, labored for peace, cared for the dying and, yes, even raised the dead.

We all face many challenges and problems. They are deeply personal, yet when joined together, they create enormous and complex chaos in the world, from our hearts to our homes to our churches and our cities. All of this chaos traces to two originating problems: sin and death. Sin, far beyond mere moral failure, describes the fundamental broken condition of every human being. Sin separates us from God and others, distorts and destroys our deepest identity as the image-bearers of God, and poses a fatal problem from which we cannot save ourselves. It results in an ever-diminishing quality of life and ultimately ends in eternal death. Because Jesus lived a life of sinless perfection, he is able to save us from sin and restore us to a right relationship with God, others, and ourselves. He did this through his sacrificial death on the cross on our behalf. Because Jesus rose from the dead, he is able to deliver us from death and bring us into a quality of life both eternal and unending.

This is the gospel of Jesus Christ: pardon from the penalty of sin, freedom from the power of sin, deliverance from the grip of death, and awakening to the supernatural empowerment of the Holy Spirit to live powerfully for the good of others and the glory of God. Jesus asks only that we acknowledge our broken selves as failed sinners, trust him as our Savior, and follow him as our Lord. Following Jesus does not mean an easy life; however, it does lead to a life of power and purpose, joy in the face of suffering, and profound, even world-changing, love for God and people.

All of this is admittedly a lot to take in. Remember, this is an invitation. Will you follow Jesus? Don't let the failings of his followers deter you. Come and see for yourself.

Here's a prayer to get you started:

> Our Father in heaven, it's me (say your name), I want to know you. I want to live an awakened life. I confess I am a sinner. I have failed myself, others, and you in many ways. I know you made me for a purpose and I want to fulfill that purpose with my one life. I want to follow Jesus Christ. Jesus, thank you for the gift of your life, death, resurrection, and ascension on my behalf. I want to walk in relationship with you as Savior and Lord. Would you lead me into the fullness and newness of life I was made for? I am ready to follow you. Come, Holy Spirit, and fill me with the love, power, and purposes of God. I pray these things by faith in the name of Jesus, amen.

It would be our privilege to help you get started and grow deeper in this awakened life of following Jesus. For some next steps and encouragements, visit seedbed.com/awaken.

How the Daily Text Works

It seems obvious to say, but the Daily Text is written every day. Mostly it is written the day before it is scheduled to release online.

Before you read further, you are cordially invited to subscribe to and receive the daily e-mail. Visit seedbed.com/dailytext to get started. Also, check out the popular Facebook group, Seedbed Daily Text.

Eventually, the daily postings become part of a Daily Text discipleship resource. That's what you hold in your hands now.

It's not exactly a Bible study, though the Bible is both the source and subject. You will learn something about the Bible along the way: its history, context, original languages, and authors. The goal is not educational in nature, but transformational. Seedbed is more interested in folks knowing Jesus than knowing *about* Jesus.

To that end, each reading begins with the definitive inspiration of the Holy Spirit, the ongoing, unfolding text of Scripture. Following that is a short and, hopefully, substantive insight from the text and some aspect of its meaning. For insight to lead to deeper influence, we turn the text into prayer. Finally, influence must run its course toward impact. This is why we ask each other questions. These questions are not designed to elicit information, but to crystallize intention.

Discipleship always leads from inspiration to intention and from attention to action.

Using the Daily Text as a Discipleship Curricular Resource for Groups

While Scripture always addresses us personally, it is not written to us individually. The content of Scripture cries out for a community to address. The Daily Text is made for discipleship in community. This resource can work in several different ways. It could be read like a traditional book, a few pages or chapters at a time. Though unadvisable, the readings could be crammed in on the night before the meeting. Keep in mind, the Daily Text is not called the Daily Text for kicks. We believe Scripture is worthy of our most focused and consistent attention. Every day. We all have misses, but let's make every day more than a noble aspiration. Let's make it our covenant with one another.

For Use with Bands

In our judgment, the best and highest use of the Daily Text is made through what we call banded discipleship. A band is a same-gender group of three to five people who read together, pray together, and meet together to become the love of God for one another and the world. With banded discipleship, the daily readings serve as a common text for the band and grist for the interpersonal conversation mill between meetings. The band meeting is reserved for the specialized activities of high-bar discipleship.

To learn more about bands and banded discipleship, visit discipleshipbands.com. Be sure to download the free *Discipleship Bands: A Practical Field Guide* or order a supply of the printed booklets online. Also be sure to explore Discipleship Bands, our native app designed specifically for the practice of banded discipleship, in the App Store or Google Play.

For Use with Classes and Small Groups

The Daily Text has also proven to be a helpful discipleship resource for a variety of small groups, from community groups to Sunday school classes. Here are some suggested guidelines for deploying the Daily Text as a resource for a small group or class setting:

1. Hearing the Text

Invite the group to settle into silence for a period of no less than one and no more than five minutes. Ask an appointed person to keep time and to read the biblical text covering the period of days since the last group meeting. Allow at least one minute of silence following the reading of the text.

2. Responding to the Text

Invite anyone from the group to respond to the reading by answering these prompts: What did you hear? What did you see? What did you otherwise sense from the Lord?

3. Sharing Insights and Implications for Discipleship

Moving in an orderly rotation (or free-for-all), invite people to share insights and implications from the week's readings.

What did you find challenging, encouraging, provocative, comforting, invasive, inspiring, corrective, affirming, guiding, or warning? Allow group conversation to proceed at will. Limit to one sharing item per turn, with multiple rounds of discussion.

4. Shaping Intentions for Prayer

Invite each person in the group to share a single discipleship intention for the week ahead. It is helpful if the intention can also be framed as a question the group can use to check in from the prior week. At each person's turn, he or she is invited to share how their intention went during the previous week. The class or group can open and close their meeting according to their established patterns.

Introduction: People Who Say Such Things . . .

All these people were still living by faith when they died. They did not receive the things promised; they only saw them and welcomed them from a distance, admitting that they were foreigners and strangers on earth. **People who say such things** show that they are looking for a country of their own. If they had been thinking of the country they had left, they would have had opportunity to return. Instead, they were longing for a better country—a heavenly one. Therefore God is not ashamed to be called their God, for he has prepared a city for them.

—Hebrews 11:13–16

"People who say such things" . . . It's a brilliant turn of phrase. But it begs the question: People who say what things?

Hebrews 11 gives us a thumbnail sketch of these people, but this banner could be lifted up over the entirety of Scripture. Who are these people and what things do they say? And, does that distinguish them from everyone else? Here are just a few examples of these people and what they say:

Ruth

But Ruth replied, "Don't urge me to leave you or to turn back from you. Where you go I will go, and where you stay I will stay. Your people will be my people and your God my God. Where you die I will die, and there I will be buried. May the LORD deal with me, be it ever so severely, if even death separates you and me." (Ruth 1:16–17)

Hannah

In her deep anguish Hannah prayed to the LORD, weeping bitterly. And she made a vow, saying, "LORD Almighty, if you will only look on your servant's misery and remember me, and not forget your servant but give her a son, then I will give him to the LORD for all the days of his life, and no razor will ever be used on his head." (1 Sam. 1:10–11)

Shadrach, Meshach, and Abednego

Shadrach, Meshach and Abednego replied to him, "King Nebuchadnezzar, we do not need to defend ourselves before you in this matter. If we are thrown into the blazing furnace, the God we serve is able to deliver us from it, and he will deliver us from Your Majesty's hand. But even if he does not, we want you to know, Your Majesty, that we will not serve your gods or worship the image of gold you have set up." (Dan. 3:16–18)

Job

"Though he slay me, yet will I hope in him." (Job 13:15a)

Mary

"I am the Lord's servant," Mary answered. "May your word to me be fulfilled." (Luke 1:38a)

Paul

I have been crucified with Christ and I no longer live, but Christ lives in me. The life I now live in the body, I live by faith in the Son of God, who loved me and gave himself for me. (Gal. 2:20)

And what of these people? Hebrews 11:16 says of them: *Instead, they were longing for a better country—a heavenly one. Therefore God is not ashamed to be called their God, for he has prepared a city for them.*

They understood themselves as *foreigners and strangers on earth.* Pay close attention though. *They were longing for a better country—a heavenly one.* This does not mean they were longing to escape the earth in order to go to heaven. No, they were longing for "on earth as it is in heaven" (see Matthew 6:10). Later in Hebrews 11:38 we read: "the world was not worthy of them." And though the world is not worthy of people who say such things, the world is desperate for them.

People who say such things have come to a place of holy discontent. They can't accept the gap between what Scripture says and the way things are. They have made the shift from being dissident malcontents who always see the problems as being out there, to being holy discontents who are willing to look within and understand how they are part of the problem. They can't accept the mess in the world nor in their own lives.

I will be forever indebted to Mrs. Betty Jane, the little lady who ran a furniture store on Main Street in Dumas, Arkansas, who was always saying such things in my hearing. I can still hear the echo of her bold voice saying, "John David, you can't do the will of God unless you know the Word of God." Then there was my mentor, Maxie Dunnam, who would say things like, "John David, there are certain things you can be and do that, apart from Jesus Christ, you will never be and do," and, "John David, there's a place in God's heart that only you can fill." Then there was my favorite Maxie saying of all time: "There are some things God either will not or cannot do until and unless his people pray."

People who say such things . . . they are all around us. To be sure, their words don't carry the weight of Scripture, but they echo its authority. That's the trick, isn't it? The secret to being a person who says such things is to first become a person who hears such things—from the people in the Bible who said such things to begin with. That's why I have written this Daily Text series: to put us in close touch with people who were in close touch with God. As you will see, we cover some ground in this book, but in the scheme of the whole Bible it's only a few legs of the journey. To borrow from Robert Frost: "[we] have miles to go before [we] sleep."

Will we become people who say such things in our lifetime? I want to, and my hunch is—you do too.

they were foreigners and strangers on earth. **People who say such things** show that they are looking for a country of

. . . Have Awakening Faith in an Age of Domesticated Religion

HEBREWS 11:1–2 | Now faith is confidence in what we hope for and assurance about what we do not see. This is what the ancients were commended for.

Consider This

Most Bible readers are familiar with the celebrated eleventh chapter of the book of Hebrews. Often called the "Hall of Faith," it offers something of a highlight reel of the great stories from across the Scriptures. It feels like an exuberant end-zone celebration with endless victory dancing.

It is nothing of the sort.

Far fewer are familiar with the last words of the preceding chapter:

> "But my righteous one will live by faith.
> And I take no pleasure
> in the one who shrinks back."
>
> But we do not belong to those who shrink back and are destroyed, but to those who have faith and are saved. (Heb. 10:38–39)

Far from a victory lap of champions, Hebrews 11 is something of a half-time speech to a losing team. These are the words of a battle-worn leader to a group of beleaguered believers who are tired, worn out, and on the brink of quitting. They believe, yet they don't see a bright future. They know a past filled with losses. They know a present screaming with pain. They cannot comprehend a future filled with hope. Victory feels like a charade. Back up a few more verses and lean into the speech:

> Remember those earlier days after you had received the light, when you endured in a great conflict full of suffering. Sometimes you were publicly exposed to insult and persecution; at other times you stood side by side with those who were so treated. You suffered along with those in prison and joyfully accepted the confiscation of your property, because you knew that you yourselves had better and lasting possessions. So do not throw away your confidence; it will be richly rewarded. (Heb. 10:32–35)

Notice how he doesn't remind them of the good times but the hard ones. He doesn't remind them of the wins but of yet more losses. He reminds them of those times when the chips were down and they didn't give up. He reminds them of the one thing that saw them through and that will see them through again: *Now faith is confidence in what we hope for and assurance about what we do not see.*

We live in an age of domesticated religion, where religious service providers readily peddle the opiates of promising prosperity and sentimental pain relief rather than helping us navigate the soul-making suffering required by the holiness of love. In this age of domesticated religion, we need a great awakening of faith. It will happen one person at a time or not at all. Methodist preacher and celebrated awakening leader E. M. Bounds once famously said, "The Church is in search of better methods. God is in search of better men." We must have better men and women. We must become great souls. Jesus stands ready to help us with Word and Spirit and all the resources of heaven. He only asks for one thing: faith. It is the one thing we must have. This is what the ancients were commended for. May it be so with us.

The Prayer

Almighty God and Father of our Lord Jesus Christ, I want to be a great soul. Awaken my longing for more of God than I presently know. Awaken my love to a passion that shreds sentiment. Awaken my faith to a fire that burns without consuming. Come, Holy Spirit, and lead us into a great awakening of faith. We pray in Jesus' name, amen.

The Questions

- Are you ready for an awakening of faith? What holds you back?

2 . . . Don't Settle for "the Faith"

HEBREWS 11:6 | And without faith it is impossible to please God, because anyone who comes to him must believe that he exists and that he rewards those who earnestly seek him.

Consider This

There's *the Faith* and then there's faith. And understanding the difference makes all the difference. This celebrated chapter of Scripture brings them together in brilliant interplay.

Let's begin with the Faith. In the opening lines of the short epistle of Jude we get this bit:

> Beloved, while I was making every effort to write you about our common salvation, I felt the necessity to write to you appealing that you contend earnestly for the faith which was once for all handed down to the saints. (Jude 1:3 NASB)

Did you catch it: "the faith"? Which faith? "The faith which was once for all handed down to the saints." Hebrews 11 stretches the faith out for us like a 360-degree horizon, looking all the way back to the creation of the world, and all the way forward to "the city with foundations, whose architect and builder is God" (Heb. 11:10), tracing the contours of a sampling of faith's impossibilities along the way.

For these next five days of immersion in this bulwark of a text, I want you to read the entirety of Hebrews 11 aloud, so your ears can hear it. That's another interesting feature of faith. According to Scripture, faith comes by hearing (see Romans 10:17).

Over the centuries, the Faith has been crystallized into creeds and catechisms, framed up in doctrinal formulations, and hammered into systematic theologies. While these things are all very good and necessary, they can and have become part of the problem for so many. For centuries now, many have given a kind of intellectual assent or a ceremonial *amen* to the Faith and considered this salute as constituting their own confession. Faith in Jesus gets reduced down to a set of propositional truths about sin, separation, death, and heaven, which the would-be believer accepts like a software agreement before joining the church and heading to the new-member luncheon.

All of this, as accurate and well-intended as it is, has the effect of domesticating religion; producing the form of faith without the power. In response, many have swung the pendulum in the opposite direction, throwing off the great anchors of the creeds and catechisms while focusing all their energy on their own personal faith experience and journey.

Hebrews 11 permits neither aberration, choosing instead to lead us into the ancient stadium of the Faith, giving us a bit of a breather in a nice luxury skybox, and then insisting that we get back on the field and into the game ourselves. Only six verses in we get this stern admonition:

And without faith it is impossible to please God, because anyone who comes to him must believe that he exists and that he rewards those who earnestly seek him.

Pay close attention to anything Scripture says is impossible. *And without faith it is impossible to please God.* This is not faith as intellectual assent, sentimental salute, or acceptance of the software agreement. This is faith as in burn-the-boats, no-turning-back, all-in abandonment to the God and Father of our Lord Jesus Christ. This is not faith as part of the herd who signed the decision card way back when. It is the faith of Abraham, Sarah, Isaac, Jacob, Mary, Joseph, Meemaw, Peepaw, Mom, Dad . . . and me.

Even me. Even you. In fact, only me and only you. That's just how down-to-the-ground and personal all this must be. You may believe the story and the stories. You may have recited the creeds ten thousand times. Heck, you may have been baptized and confirmed. Still here's the point:

And without faith it is impossible to please God, because anyone who comes to him must believe that he exists and that he rewards those who earnestly seek him.

So, Christian, let me ask you: Do you have faith? Do you believe God exists and that he rewards those who earnestly seek him? And even as I ask you these questions, it occurs to me just how pointless the exercise is. There is a better question. It is the real question faith asks us today, right now:

Are you earnestly seeking him?

The Prayer

Father of Abraham, Isaac, and Jacob, God of our fathers and mothers, awaken us . . . No, awaken *me* to the real faith . . . not the form of faith. Don't let me hide behind the faith of the church or of anyone else. I want to grow in my faith, so whatever it takes, Lord, let faith arise in me. Come, Holy Spirit, and train my spirit to earnestly seek after you. We pray in the name of our Lord and King Jesus Christ, the pioneer and perfecter of our faith, amen.

The Question

- Stay with the question: Are you earnestly seeking him? How do you know?

. . . Move from Commitment to Consecration

3

HEBREWS 11:13–16 | All these people were still living by faith when they died. They did not receive the things promised; they only saw them and welcomed them from a distance, admitting that they were foreigners and strangers on earth. People who say such things show that they are looking for a country of their own. If they had been thinking of the country they had left, they would have had opportunity to return. Instead, they were longing for a better country—a heavenly one. Therefore God is not ashamed to be called their God, for he has prepared a city for them.

Consider This

Take a few minutes now and read Hebrews 11, the entire chapter, aloud. As you read, I'll be running an interpretive banner up the flagpole of our collective souls with these words: *earnestly seeking him*. And as you do this, know it is an act of worship in and of itself to read the Holy Word of God aloud. These are the very words that remake the world, and they never return to him void.

You will remember from yesterday's reading this word from Hebrews 11:6 about God rewarding "those who earnestly seek him." Let's spend another minute on this concept. It is important to understand that earnestly seeking God does not mean revving up the engines on what you are already doing. It can't be reduced to getting up an hour earlier, reading a chapter longer, praying a bit bolder, and otherwise trying to do more to be a better and more devoted Christian. Let's call this the struggle of striving.

Earnestly seeking him is something altogether different. It requires a different mentality and mind-set. We must shift from the ascent mode of striving for God into the descent mentality of abandonment to God. Faith does not require striving; it invites outright surrender.

Some weeks ago I was with my close friend and constant encourager, Brian. We were talking about eating healthy when the conversation turned to sugar. He said something to me that lodged a splinter in my soul. He said, "John David, 99 percent is hell. One hundred percent is heaven. Your big problem with sugar is you bounce around with your food choices between 1 percent and 99 percent, but you have never gone to 100 percent. Once you go 100 percent in, you will be done with sugar and there are no more choices."

Let's just say the dominoes in my soul began to fall. One to 99 percent is the continuum of striving—the country called "commitment." One hundred percent is the zone of surrender—the country called "consecration." Like a New Year's resolution, striving and commitment are seductive, all at once requiring enormous effort on our part while keeping us 100-percent in control. It's why they seldom survive January. We never left the old country. We just doubled down our efforts on trying to find a better way in an old place. Surrender and consecration take us out of the old country. They don't show us a better way, but a better country. We are no longer in control at all, but we have ceded our control to a sovereign beyond ourselves. We now belong to Jesus, which brings meaning to the originating creed of our faith: Jesus is Lord!

The greatest proverbial leap of faith is not from unbelief to belief, but from striving to surrender and from commitment to consecration. It is to move from the continuum of 1 percent to 99 percent to the country of 100 percent. It is not about revving up our commitment, but giving up our control. Now here's the interesting part: we don't actually leave anywhere or anyone behind. Though we are still surrounded by the old country, we begin to see the new creation springing up everywhere, both from a distance and yet gloriously up close. We discover life, not according to a better way, but by a new way entirely. We become citizens of heaven with an earthly address, doing things we never imagined possible with people we thought were too good to be true.

There's so much to be said here, but I've got to land the plane for today. Now read today's passage in light of these ponderings and see what you see:

All these people were still living by faith when they died. They did not receive the things promised; they only saw them and welcomed them from a distance, admitting that they were foreigners and strangers on earth. People who say such things show that they are looking for a country of their own. If they had been thinking of the country they had left, they would have had opportunity to return. Instead, they were longing for a better country—a heavenly one. Therefore God is not ashamed to be called their God, for he has prepared a city for them.

The Prayer

Our Father in heaven, here I am, a citizen of your kingdom living in the midst of the kingdoms of this world. Awaken me to the glorious possibilities of this life of faith. Lead me out of the slavery of my own committed-ness and into the new land of consecrated-ness. I want to be done with my striving so that I might lay down my life in trusting surrender to you. Come, Holy Spirit, and show me this new way of earnestly seeking after you. We pray in the name of our Lord and King, Jesus Christ, the pioneer and perfecter of our faith, amen.

The Questions

- So how about it? Are you a striver? Does this make sense to you: the difference between striving and surrender; the difference between commitment and consecration; the difference between being the sovereign of your own self and ceding control over to the sovereignty of God?

. . . Trade in Transactional Faith for Transcendent Faith

4

HEBREWS 11:8–12 | By faith Abraham, when called to go to a place he would later receive as his inheritance, obeyed and went, even though he did not know where he was going. By faith he made his home in the promised land like a stranger in a foreign country; he lived in tents, as did Isaac and Jacob, who were heirs with him of the same promise. For he was looking forward to the city with foundations, whose architect and builder is God. And by faith even Sarah, who was past childbearing age, was enabled to bear children because she considered him faithful who had made the promise. And so from this one man, and he as good as dead, came descendants as numerous as the stars in the sky and as countless as the sand on the seashore.

Consider This

Yesterday we talked about the difference between striving and surrender and between commitment and consecration. Today I want to make a parallel kind of comparison and contrast many will find challenging and even off-putting.

There are at least two kinds of faith. The first faith is transactional faith. It can be brought down to two words: "Help me!" We find ourselves in a messed-up, mixed-up, chaotic world plagued by sin and death, and it touches every aspect of our lives, families, and communities. However, in the unparalleled prosperity of the United States of America, we can almost manage to insulate ourselves from our need through some combination of achievement and addiction. We vacillate between education and entertainment in an endless quest for the ephemeral experiences of the so-called good life, turning to the gods of self-help when they seem to suit our situation.

Somewhere along the way, either through the echoes of our childhood churches or faith-filled grandparents or some kind of midlife train wreck or tragedy, we wake up to our deep, insatiable need. By the mercy of God, we are found by the grace of God, and we wake up to his mysterious, transformational presence in this tragic world. We discover the two words and we begin speaking them in direct speech to God: "Help me!"

And God helps us. We develop a transactional faith, which grows into a personal sense of relationship with God and we begin to grow in the grace of God. We learn to depend on God as we bring him our needs and the needs of others, crying out with ever-growing confidence, "Help me!" While this is a good and necessary stage of faith, most people never go beyond it. We get stuck, arrested in development, with lives consumed by the constant cares and concerns of our broken lives in this broken world. We do our best, striving to be committed, living in this old country on its terms while calling on the resources of heaven to help us endure it. Faith can become weary and even stale in this old country as we learn to endure what we can't understand and to trust what we cannot see.

It brings us to the second kind of faith. Let's call it transcendent faith. It, too, can be brought down to two words: "Have me!" This is the faith of surrender and consecration. Again, the greatest proverbial leap of faith is not from unbelief to belief, but from striving to surrender and from commitment to consecration. This is the faith of abandon. It comes from a deep place of holy discontent; an unwillingness to accept the world on any set of terms other than those of Father, Son, and Holy Spirit. It comes from an unwillingness to tolerate the gap between the promises and possibilities we see in the Word of God and the devastation and desolation in the world we live in.

Perhaps the best summary of transcendent faith comes from Paul's letter to the Galatian Christians when he said, "I have been crucified with Christ and I no longer live, but Christ lives in me. The life I now live in the body, I live by faith in the Son of God, who loved me and gave himself for me" (Gal. 2:20). This way of transcendent faith is available to anyone but few take the invitation, and yet this is the faith that precedes great awakenings. This is the faith of impossible things. Hebrews 11, indeed, the whole of Scripture, overflows with portraits of "Have me!" faith. Consider the contours of such faith with a careful rereading of today's text:

> By faith Abraham, when called to go to a place he would later receive as his inheritance, obeyed and went, even though he did not know where he was going. By faith he made his home in the promised land like a stranger in a foreign country; he lived in tents, as did Isaac and Jacob, who were heirs with him of the same promise. For he was looking forward to the city with foundations, whose architect and builder is God. And by faith even Sarah, who was past childbearing age, was enabled to bear children because she considered him faithful who had made the promise. And so from this one man, and he as good as dead, came descendants as numerous as the stars in the sky and as countless as the sand on the seashore.

The Prayer

Our Father in heaven, here I am, thankful for and yet weary of transactional faith. I want this transcendent faith. Thank you for helping me over and over and over again. I will always ask you to help me. However, I am ready for a new prayer. I am ready to say to you, "Have me!" I want my life to be a transcendent touchpoint for your life. Come, Holy Spirit, and show me this new and "ever-newing" way of faith. Let it be said of us that we walk in a way of faith that produces impossible things. We pray in the name of our Lord and King, Jesus Christ, the pioneer and perfecter of our faith, amen.

The Questions

- How do you see the difference between transactional and transcendent faith; between the "Help me!" prayer and the "Have me!" prayer?

. . . Are Ready for the Next Step

5

HEBREWS 11:1–2, 13 | Now faith is confidence in what we hope for and assurance about what we do not see. This is what the ancients were commended for. . . .

All these people were still living by faith when they died. They did not receive the things promised; they only saw them and welcomed them from a distance, admitting that they were foreigners and strangers on earth.

Consider This

We have all heard the reference of blind faith. Even Scripture seems to nod to this notion. Paul says to the Corinthian Christians, "for we walk by faith, not by sight" (2 Cor. 5:7 ESV).

It has a certain logic, but to walk by faith is not to be blind. Walking by faith means seeing with a vision beyond mere eyesight. Faith is actually the opposite of blindness. It means super vision.

The Bible is the revealed record of those sinners, saints, angels, and apostles who saw the vision and abandoned their lives to see its fulfillment. Faith is not blind, if by "blind," we mean unable to see.

Now faith is confidence in what we hope for and assurance about what we do not see. This is what the ancients were commended for.

The problem comes when we adopt a concept of faith built around the limits of what we can see with our eyes. We live imprisoned by our challenging circumstances, turning to God for help and relief according to the level of our desperation. When things work out we consider God has heard our prayers, and when they don't we chalk it up to some other reason God must have or a bigger plan.

This is blind faith. This is the realm of transactional faith. It is "Help me" faith, which—I repeat—is not bad, but is only meant to be a stage of faith we pass through rather than get stuck in. If we are honest with ourselves, the overwhelming quest of this kind of faith is to help us make it through "this life" in "this world" and go to heaven when we die. This kind of faith bounces between the boundaries of prosperity on one side and poverty on the other; battling between peace and perseverance, depending on the day. And in between we invest in the stock market, buy lottery tickets, purchase insurance policies, go to church, pray, and try to be good citizens. In other words, we do our best to build our homes in this world, making the best of a broken situation, and somehow our faith gets us through. To be sure, this is faith, but it is a domesticated faith at best.

This is not the faith the ancients were commended for. The ancients were commended for a visionary faith that could see past the veil of what was visible to the eye and into the glorious realm of God's revelation. The ancients were commended for faith-walking their ordinary lives up to that cliff and jumping off. It's right there in verse 13:

All these people were still living by faith when they died. They did not receive the things promised; they only saw them and welcomed them from a distance, admitting that they were foreigners and strangers on earth.

To be a foreigner and stranger on earth does not mean biding one's time until escaping to heaven. It means to live boldly by faith, contending for the beatific vision of "on earth as it is in heaven" (see Matthew 6:10). It means to take one's stand on this soil and live as a transcendent beacon of all the promises and possibilities of God in Jesus' name, by the power of the Holy Spirit, right here and right now. It looks like two retirees the world would consider "as good as dead" who dare to look up at the stars and believe the time they have left could be enough to change the world. It looks like a family building a boat in the middle of a desert. It looks like a kid with a slingshot facing a giant. It looks like an army armed with trumpets, torches, and clay pots.

I realize I may be scaring half of the Daily Text community away with this message. I don't mean to. I just want you to wake up. I love you too much to let you hit the snooze bar again. The biggest impediment to you and I waking up to the next step of faith God has for us is that we are pretty sure we are already awake.

We live in an age increasingly anesthetized by darkness. We are all affected. It will take a great awakening to turn the tide. It will take mountain-moving faith. Some of you reading have already begun to stand up and say, "Here I am, Lord. Send me" (see Isaiah 6:8). And to be sure, I don't have in mind hundreds of people quitting their jobs, becoming professional Christians, and "going into the ministry." That's a far too predictable and benign strategy for the task at hand.

The truth is, I am not writing to all of you today. I am not even writing to some of you. I am writing to one of you. Because when just one person stands up and steps forward into this kind of invitation, millions wake up.

The only question you have to answer today is: Am I writing to you?

The Prayer

Our Father in heaven, part of me is offended by these words and yet that same part of me is challenged to the core of my being. I want to dismiss this as impractical and unreasonable, yet something deeper tells me to lean in. I hardly grasp this, yet I will lean in and say, "Speak, LORD, for your servant is listening" (1 Sam. 3:9). We pray in the name of our

Lord and King, Jesus Christ, the pioneer and perfecter of our faith, amen.

The Question

- So am I writing to you today?

. . . Speak the Hardest Words in the Hardest Times

6

MATTHEW 27:46 | About three in the afternoon Jesus cried out in a loud voice, *"Eli, Eli, lema sabachthani?"* (which means "My God, my God, why have you forsaken me?").

Consider This

"People who say such things . . ."

Hmm. We see these words the first time in the Twenty-Second Psalm, from the mouth of David, the man after God's own heart, "My God, my God, why have you forsaken me?" (v. 1).

Who says this? Only everybody who has ever lived—from the fifteen-year-old whose girlfriend just abandoned him for another suitor to the terminal breast cancer patient in room #204—the felt-ness of forsakenness by God is a very human reality. Though people in the grip of loss or the jaws of death have others close around them, they feel forsaken by God, because only God could have changed the awful outcome they suffer. Whether they believe in God or not and whether their lung cancer is from smoking two packs a day for forty years, they hope (if not, expect) God to do something. So in one sense, every kind of person, at one time or another, says such a thing as, "My God, my God, why have you forsaken me?"

There is a second group of people, though, who say such things. These are the particular people who have abandoned their life to God in an extraordinary way. You have followed Jesus all the way there and back. You are people after God's own heart: poor in spirit, strong in faith, meek, humble, courageous, generous—all of that and more. Through some turn of events and clash of circumstances, you find yourself feeling forsaken by God. It's not turning out like you thought. The chemo is not working. They don't want you as their leader any longer. The marriage failed. The depression is not lifting. You never gave up on God, but it sure feels like God has given up on you.

About three in the afternoon Jesus cried out in a loud voice, "Eli, Eli, lema sabachthani?" *(which means "My God, my God, why have you forsaken me?").*

People who say such things are Jesus' people. These people keep it real. You refuse to put a fresh coat of paint on a rotten piece of furniture. You understand that though your feelings may deceive you, your situation is real and cannot be denied. You understand the importance of crying out, as the text says, "in a loud voice."

About three in the afternoon Jesus cried out in a loud voice, "Eli, Eli, lema sabachthani?" *(which means "My God, my God, why have you forsaken me?").*

Because you know God, you know God can handle your dissonance. In fact, you know God would rather you be real about your dissonance than stuff it into the recesses of your soul. People who say such things are way deep into the deal— so deep, they know there is no deal—only a promise: "I am with you always, to the very end of the age" (Matt. 28:20), which means through it all, no matter what.

You know it will not always seem like he is with you, even to the point of feeling forsaken, because the one who made the promise not to forsake us was the one who felt the most forsaken. All of this is because people who say such things know one thing is a matter of settled doctrine: on the other side of the cross is the resurrection. Psalm 22 fittingly closes with these words: "He has done it!" (v. 31).

It's why you are one of these kinds of people who say such things.

The Prayer

Father, at any given moment I know it's going to be me or someone I know or someone I know about who is feeling forsaken by you. Give me the grace to have and hold this very real feeling, and the grace to let others hold it. In fact, show me what it looks like to hold them just where they are and to resist the need I may have to comfort them with some truthful platitude that is less then helpful. We all know you never leave or forsake us, yet sometimes it's in your felt absence that we learn to cry out in a loud voice, which leads us further into your presence than we would ever have known apart from feeling forsaken. Come, Holy Spirit, and train me to be one of these kinds of people. I pray in Jesus' name, amen.

The Questions

- Do you have a "My God, my God, why have you forsaken me" story? How did it go? Have you told it?

7   . . . Take the Road Less Traveled

GENESIS 13:8–9 | So Abram said to Lot, "Let's not have any quarreling between you and me, or between your herders and mine, for we are close relatives. Is not the whole land before you? Let's part company. If you go to the left, I'll go to the right; if you go to the right, I'll go to the left."

Consider This

Let's back up a couple thousand years—all the way back to the almost beginning—back to Abraham (a.k.a. Abram). God called him to leave everything he had ever known to pursue a future beyond his imagining based on the promise of God's Word. Genesis 12:4 may be the most consequential text in all of Scripture: "So Abram went, as the LORD had told him; and

Lot went with him. Abram was seventy-five years old when he set out from Harran."

Three side points: (1) simple obedience, (2) take others with you, and (3) God doesn't accept, "I'm too old" excuses.

The relatives apparently ran into conflict, as family is wont to do. At last their respective tribes weren't jiving. It brings us to today's text:

So Abram said to Lot, "Let's not have any quarreling between you and me, or between your herders and mine, for we are close relatives. Is not the whole land before you? Let's part company. If you go to the left, I'll go to the right; if you go to the right, I'll go to the left."

People who say such things are abundance people. You are openhanded, trusting, and generous. Because you know what it means to freely receive something, you also know what it means to freely give it away. People like this are not afraid of getting the short end of the stick. You don't live in scarcity, even when it seems like resources are extremely scarce. You know there's always more than meets the eye; even when things like this happen: "Lot looked around and saw that the whole plain of the Jordan toward Zoar was well watered, like the garden of the LORD, like the land of Egypt. (This was before the LORD destroyed Sodom and Gomorrah.) So Lot chose for himself the whole plain of the Jordan and set out toward the east. The two men parted company" (Gen. 13:10–11).

Abram took the road less traveled and it made all the difference. Sometimes, maybe even often, faith looks a lot like trusting deference. It looks like being in charge and surprisingly taking the back seat, conceding the advantage to someone else. Lot took the other road, and it did not work out—to put it mildly. Lot took the "garden of the Lord" land and it turned into a wasteland. Do the names Sodom and Gomorrah ring a bell?

And somewhere in here there's a word to families in conflict, maybe even brothers who are struggling to get along. Take a page from Abram's playbook. Be a person who says such things. Be the bigger brother.

So what about Abram? Sooner or later, here's what happens to abundance people:

> The Lord said to Abram after Lot had parted from him, "Look around from where you are, to the north and south, to the east and west. All the land that you see I will give to you and your offspring forever. I will make your offspring like the dust of the earth, so that if anyone could count the dust, then your offspring could be counted. Go, walk through the length and breadth of the land, for I am giving it to you." (Gen. 13:14–17)

It's why you want to be a person who says such things.

The Prayer

Father, I want to be a person who trusts you explicitly and implicitly. I want to be such a person who could prefer to apparently lose a conflict in the interest of winning the peace. Show me this way of wise deference to others, of yielding the front-row parking space, or the front-row seat, or the advantage at work, or in a family estate, or maybe even a church, or a whole denomination. And give me the joy of seeing your faithfulness in leading me to something far greater than I might have imagined. Root out all the scarcity-thinking that remains in me. I want to be an abundance person. Come, Holy Spirit, and train me to be one of these kinds of people. I pray in Jesus' name, amen.

The Questions

- Do any situations come to mind from your own life from reading today's text? Are you more of a scarcity person or an abundance person at this point in your life and faith? How can you grow toward abundance?

. . . Trade Incredulity for Inquisitiveness

8

GENESIS 17:17 | Abraham fell facedown; he laughed and said to himself, "Will a son be born to a man a hundred years old? Will Sarah bear a child at the age of ninety?"

Consider This

Incredulity.

It's that moment when something incredible actually falls off the cliff and becomes "incred-uble." To be fair, the word *incredible* actually means impossible to believe. And *increduble*, though it's a rogue word, strikes me as the perfect word. It describes the collision of something incredible and something dubious. In television parlance, they call this, "jumping the shark." A television show jumps the shark when the plot turns in such a ridiculously absurd way, most sensible viewers abandon ship. It becomes incredulous—like the one when God told one-hundred-year-old Abraham that he and his ninety-year-old wife would have a baby.

> God also said to Abraham, "As for Sarai your wife, you are no longer to call her Sarai; her name will be Sarah. I will bless her and will surely give you a son by her. I will bless her so that she will be the mother of nations; kings of peoples will come from her." (Gen. 17:15–16)

Abraham literally fell out of his chair laughing. Don't believe me?

Abraham fell facedown; he laughed and said to himself, "Will a son be born to a man a hundred years old? Will Sarah bear a child at the age of ninety?"

People who say such things demonstrate a willingness to move from incredulity to inquiry. They fall out laughing at the ridiculous notion, yet they dare to crack the door, to entertain it by asking themselves the questions: *"Will a son be born to a man a hundred years old? Will Sarah bear a child at the age of ninety?"*

I preached recently at a series of meetings. In one of the messages I spoke on the passage in Acts 3 where Peter and John famously heal the beggar who was "lame from birth" (Acts 3:2). Peter said, "Silver or gold I do not have, but what I do have I give you. In the name of Jesus Christ of Nazareth, walk" (v. 6). I remarked at how incredible it would be to do such a thing. After the message an older woman approached me with a word. She said, "You will be part of miraculous work like that." I laughed. I found it incredulous. Weeks later, I still mull this over, asking myself: *Will I command the lame to walk in Jesus' name?* To ask the question is to risk the answer. I am moving from incredulity to inquisitive.

It's okay to believe the miraculous is too incredible to be possible—for a minute. It's okay to find the possibilities of God incredulous and inaccessible to yourself—for a while. The one thing you can't do is to dismiss them.

There are some people out there whose doctrinal belief system separates the Bible from now; as in, that was then but this is now. There are plenty of people whose faith (and heart) has been broken by God's apparent failure to come through for them. Whether your incredulity at the laughable possibilities of God (even in your own life) comes from a place of your doctrine or your brokenness or even your indifference matters not.

The question is: Will you crack the door of your mind and heart to the question? Will you risk the disruption to your doctrine, the pain of yet more disappointment, or the inter-ruption of your indifference? You may laugh it off, but will you trade in your incredulity for inquisitiveness and become a person who says such things?

Abraham fell facedown; he laughed and said to himself, "Will a son be born to a man a hundred years old? Will Sarah bear a child at the age of ninety?"

The Prayer

Father, I want to be a person who says such things. When it comes to my faith in you, I want to count the cost, yet I want to be an uncalculated risk-taker. I would rather err on the side of leaning into your possibilities, even the far-fetched and miraculous ones, than to play it safe on the sidelines. Where are you inviting me to ask myself about the challenging thing you may be saying to me? Right now, so much of it seems incredulous. Open my heart to inquisitiveness, to ask the question, to risk the disappointment of faith, even the disruption of my well-laid plans for my well-planned life. Come, Holy Spirit, and train me to be one of these kinds of people. I pray in Jesus' name, amen.

The Questions

- So what might be the incredulous possibility the Spirit is identifying in your life? It doesn't need to be miraculous or even grand—just a place where you are disinclined to believe. What might the question look like for you today?

9 . . . Have Audacity

GENESIS 18:22–28 | The men turned away and went toward Sodom, but Abraham remained standing before the LORD. Then Abraham approached him and said: "Will you sweep away the righteous with the wicked? What if there are fifty righteous people in the city? Will you really sweep it away and not spare

the place for the sake of the fifty righteous people in it? Far be it from you to do such a thing—to kill the righteous with the wicked, treating the righteous and the wicked alike. Far be it from you! Will not the Judge of all the earth do right?"

The LORD said, "If I find fifty righteous people in the city of Sodom, I will spare the whole place for their sake."

Then Abraham spoke up again: "Now that I have been so bold as to speak to the Lord, though I am nothing but dust and ashes, what if the number of the righteous is five less than fifty? Will you destroy the whole city for lack of five people?"

"If I find forty-five there," he said, "I will not destroy it."

Consider This

Audacity.

That's the word. It means someone who is so bold in their approach they are willing to risk causing offense. Yesterday we witnessed Abraham's incredulity. Today we see his audacity.

Catching up with the story line: Abraham received a visit from three strangers, who carried the character of angelic beings in the appearance of men. They announced the coming of the promised son to Abraham and Sarah. Afterward they headed on to their next assignment, which included the complete and utter destruction of Sodom and Gomorrah.

The Lord decided to confide their mission to Abraham. We enter in two verses prior to today's text:

> Then the LORD said, "The outcry against Sodom and Gomorrah is so great and their sin so grievous that I

will go down and see if what they have done is as bad as the outcry that has reached me. If not, I will know." (Gen. 18:20–21)

Here's where Abe gets audacious:

Then Abraham approached him and said: "Will you sweep away the righteous with the wicked?

That's bold. Who does that? This is *the Lord* he addressed. This is the same guy who tried to pass off his wife as his sister in order to save his own bacon—which raises another good point. We are all in process; an inconsistent mix of magnificence and mess. Anyway, back to Abraham. He knew his nephew Lot and their whole clan were in imminent danger, so he intervened. Better yet—he interceded. That may be the better word. He stood before the God of heaven and earth on behalf of Lot.

What if there are fifty righteous people in the city? Will you really sweep it away and not spare the place for the sake of the fifty righteous people in it?

Three questions and counting. Abraham appealed to God on the basis of God's character.

Far be it from you to do such a thing—to kill the righteous with the wicked, treating the righteous and the wicked alike. Far be it from you! Will not the Judge of all the earth do right?"

God called his bluff and agreed to save the cities for fifty righteous souls. Small problem: Abraham was bluffing. He knew fifty was a pipe dream. Abe's audacity goes to the next level.

Then Abraham spoke up again: "Now that I have been so bold as to speak to the Lord, though I am nothing but dust and ashes, what if the number of the righteous is five less than fifty? Will you destroy the whole city for lack of five people?"

Notice how Abraham's audacity doesn't spring from his own strength or fortitude. He knows he is dust. His audacity doesn't come from the righteousness of his cause. This whole affair became something of an auction in reverse until Abraham finally locked in the deal at ten righteous people—who ultimately could not be found. Abraham's audacious appeal does not spring from his own compassion or inner conviction that he must do something. Abraham's audacity anchors itself 100-percent in the compassionate nature and righteous character of God.

People who say such things possess an audacity beyond activism. Your audacity comes not from the weight of your character or the justice of your cause, it comes from the heart of your God.

The Prayer

Father, I want to have this kind of audacity, yet I fear any boldness I may have is generated by my own force of personality or personal conviction. I know I am mere dust. And yet I know you. I want to learn to pray not on the strength of my sincerity, but on the basis of your character. Show me how to pray with audacity on the basis of who you are rather than on the intensity (or lack thereof) of who I am. Come, Holy

Spirit, and train me to be one of these kinds of people. I pray in Jesus' name, amen.

The Question

- How might this kind of audacity change your approach to speaking with God about difficult situations in your life and in the world around us?

10 . . . Walk in Unwavering Faith

GENESIS 22:1–5 | Some time later God tested Abraham. He said to him, "Abraham!"

"Here I am," he replied.

Then God said, "Take your son, your only son, whom you love—Isaac—and go to the region of Moriah. Sacrifice him there as a burnt offering on a mountain I will show you."

Early the next morning Abraham got up and loaded his donkey. He took with him two of his servants and his son Isaac. When he had cut enough wood for the burnt offering, he set out for the place God had told him about. On the third day Abraham looked up and saw the place in the distance. He said to his servants, "Stay here with the donkey while I and the boy go over there. We will worship and then we will come back to you."

Consider This

Unwavering.

He said to his servants, "Stay here with the donkey while I and the boy go over there. We will worship and then we will come back to you."

With these words of Abraham, God reveals to us a rarified quality of unwavering faith that is nothing short of breathtaking.

Then God said, "Take your son, your only son, whom you love—Isaac—and go to the region of Moriah. Sacrifice him there as a burnt offering on a mountain I will show you."

Did God really just tell Abraham to sacrifice his son? Where is Abraham's incredulity now? Where did Abraham's audacious attitude go? Why isn't he questioning and pushing back? Instead, he unflinchingly obeys. Of all times for a time-out, this would be it.

Everything is set. Wood is chopped. Fire in hand. Knife at the ready. Then we get this:

He said to his servants, "Stay here with the donkey while I and the boy go over there. We will worship and then we will come back to you."

Abraham knew. It was as though God quietly messaged Abraham somewhere along the way on this three-day walk: "I need you to know that I know. I know that you know Isaac was never in the slightest danger. This was never about Isaac. It was never about me. It was about you, Abraham. These loyalties are not conflicting unless they are competing. Abraham, your loyalty to and love for Isaac, the gift, is grounded in and flows from your loyalty to and love for me, but it can never be the other way around. The minute the gift gets separated from the Giver is the moment you become the god, and from there it's only a matter of time until everything goes off the rails."

Abraham's lineage, his security, and his legacy were not in his son, but in his God. God knew this, but Abraham needed to know it. Would Abraham trust God in a way that could cost him everything? Would he place the gift back in the hands of the Giver—and in so doing, would he offer himself? Sometimes it takes the prospect of a burnt offering to get to the place of a living sacrifice.

The writer of Hebrews put it this way: "Abraham reasoned that God could even raise the dead, and so in a manner of speaking he did receive Isaac back from death" (11:19).

Here's an example: God blesses a person with wealth. They know it has come from God, and they share it freely and generously. There is a fluid flow of blessing, of giving and receiving, of generosity and gratitude. Over time, though, little by little, they start to hold back, to play it safe—you know—conserve. As wealth grows larger, faith has a way of shrinking smaller. Loyalty to God slowly slips as love of money seductively surges. Somewhere along the way the focus slowly and almost imperceptibly shifts from devotion to God to dealing with the money. We want to think trust will grow and giving will become easier as blessing increases. It does not. It gets harder—because we think we have more to lose—which is why we must grow deeper in love with God. Our heart-level bond with God must become gut level.

This is the cross—where our loyalties become level-set, our loves become prioritized, and our lives become most truly alive. When we lay our lives down as an offering, we can receive them back from the dead as a living sacrifice. This is the place where our worship ceases to be something we do and rises up in to who we are becoming. We become transcendent beacons of God's glory—and our stories in time become ensconced in eternity.

He said to his servants, "Stay here with the donkey while I and the boy go over there. We will worship and then we will come back to you."

People who say such things become so confident in the love of God they grow to be unflinching in their faith. Their faith is no longer anchored in their commitment or even in their beliefs. It has become anchored in God himself, and through people like these he delights to surprise the world with the new wine of his kingdom.

The Prayer

Father, I want to have unwavering faith and yet, if that is my focus, I will miss the mark. In order to have unwavering faith, I must have you. I must know you more. Bring me to understand your unwavering love, affection, and loyalty to me. By your Spirit, increase the bond between us. I pray in Jesus' name, amen.

The Questions

- Where in your life have the gifts of God gotten separated from God the Giver and created competing loyalties? Could it be your career? Your family? Your wealth?

11 ... Show Us How Faith Works

GENESIS 24:1–9 | Abraham was now very old, and the LORD had blessed him in every way. He said to the senior servant in his household, the one in charge of all that he had, "Put your hand under my thigh. I want you to swear by the LORD, the God of heaven and the God of earth, that you will not get a wife for my son from the daughters of the Canaanites, among whom I am living, but will go to my country and my own relatives and get a wife for my son Isaac."

The servant asked him, "What if the woman is unwilling to come back with me to this land? Shall I then take your son back to the country you came from?"

"Make sure that you do not take my son back there," Abraham said. "The LORD, the God of heaven, who brought me out of my father's household and my native land and who spoke to me and promised me on oath, saying, 'To your offspring I will give this land'—he will send his angel before you so that you can get a wife for my son from there. If the woman is unwilling to come back with you, then you will be released from this oath of mine. Only do not take my son back there." So the servant put his hand under the thigh of his master Abraham and swore an oath to him concerning this matter.

Consider This

Observe the blessed outcome of an obedient life.

Abraham was now very old, and the Lord had blessed him in every way.

Abraham didn't rest in this. He lived by faith in the promises of God to the very end. He called his servant and enlisted him in the cause. He sent the servant back to his homeland to get a wife for Isaac. Two things Abraham knew: first, Isaac's wife needed to come from Abraham's homeland and clan. Second, Isaac had to stay in the land of the Canaanites which the Lord had promised to Abraham's descendants.

Abraham lived between a promise and its fulfillment.

"The Lord, the God of heaven, who brought me out of my father's household and my native land and who spoke to me and promised me on oath, saying, 'To your offspring I will give this land'—he will send his angel before you so that you can get a wife for my son from there. If the woman is unwilling to come back with you, then you will be released from this oath of mine. Only do not take my son back there."

People who say such things show us the very essence of faith. As far as faith is concerned, a promise from God is money in the bank. It is as good as fulfilled. Faith, in fact, doesn't hope in the promise but actually moves as though it is already done.

Abraham knew by faith the servant would find a wife and yet he was not sure it would work out like he thought. This potential wife would have a will of her own. Maybe she would not come back with the servant. In other words, God's will is God's will, yet a person's free will is just that—their free will. Abraham asked the servant to swear him an oath, yet he gave the servant an out clause.

Abraham extended his faith as far as he could—which was complete dependence on God—and yet if it didn't work out like he thought, he still completely depended on God to work it out in some other way he couldn't yet see.

In the matter of God's will, everything depends on God, yet the free will of people can pose enormous complexities in how God's will ultimately gets worked out. People can thwart God's plan, but they can't change his will. God always has another plan and another one after that. We can't control the outcome or even the process. We can only be obedient as far as we can understand and see. We seek wisdom from God by faith and then we set things in motion by obedience. From there we let things unfold, trusting the process and outcome and all the possible (and even impossible) contingencies to God.

God's will is fixed, yet his ways are fluid. We are not responsible for the choices of others—only our obedience to our best understanding of God's will and our best discernment of the ways God works with us. It requires us to move all at once with a humble boldness and yet a faith-filled tentativeness.

We, too, live between a promise and its fulfillment.

People who say such things show us how to do it.

The Prayer

Father, I want to be a person who says such things. I want to be a person who trusts your will and who obeys your plan and yet who trusts the process and the outcome to you. Forgive me for my need to be in control. You are in control. Give me the courage to have the faith to play my part, whether it makes sense to me or not. Train my spirit to be boldly confident that your will will, in fact, be done, yet wildly open to how you will bring it about. Come, Holy Spirit, and train me to be such a person of faith. I pray in Jesus' name, amen.

The Questions

- God's will is fixed, yet his ways are fluid. How do you understand, agree with, disagree with, and grapple with this statement? How do you relate to this notion of the contingencies and complexities of how God's will gets worked out in our lives?

. . . Seek Confirmation Rather than Proof

12

GENESIS 24:10–21 | Then the servant left, taking with him ten of his master's camels loaded with all kinds of good things from his master. He set out for Aram Naharaim and made his way to the town of Nahor. He had the camels kneel down near the well outside the town; it was toward evening, the time the women go out to draw water.

Then he prayed, "Lord, God of my master Abraham, make me successful today, and show kindness to my master Abraham. See, I am standing beside this spring, and the daughters of the townspeople are coming out to draw water. May it be that when I say to a young woman, 'Please let down your jar that I may have a drink,' and she says, 'Drink, and I'll water your camels too'—let her be the one you have chosen for your servant Isaac. By this I will know that you have shown kindness to my master."

Before he had finished praying, Rebekah came out with her jar on her shoulder. She was the daughter of Bethuel son of Milkah, who was the wife of Abraham's brother Nahor. The woman was very beautiful, a virgin; no man had ever slept with her. She went down to the spring, filled her jar and came up again.

The servant hurried to meet her and said, "Please give me a little water from your jar."

"Drink, my lord," she said, and quickly lowered the jar to her hands and gave him a drink.

After she had given him a drink, she said, "I'll draw water for your camels too, until they have had enough to drink." So she quickly emptied her jar into the trough, ran back to the well to draw more water, and drew enough for all his camels. Without saying a word, the man watched her closely to learn whether or not the Lord had made his journey successful.

Consider This

Abraham's servant had his work cut out for him. The pressure was on to find the perfect wife for Isaac. This likely made weeding the garden look like fun! He didn't devise a strategic plan. He didn't make a checklist. He asked the Lord for a confirming sign:

"May it be that when I say to a young woman, 'Please let down your jar that I may have a drink,' and she says, 'Drink, and I'll water your camels too'—let her be the one you have chosen for your servant Isaac. By this I will know that you have shown kindness to my master."

It was not a random sign, like a woman in a red dress. It was a bit of an exceptional sign. He was looking for a woman of extraordinary character—one who would take the rest of her night to serve a complete stranger in a very strenuous fashion (i.e., watering ten camels).

And what do you know—it happened—just as he asked.

Before he had finished praying, Rebekah came out with her jar on her shoulder. . . . After she had given him a drink, she said, "I'll draw water for your camels too, until they have had enough to drink." So she quickly emptied her jar into the trough, ran back to the well to draw more water, and drew enough for all his camels.

There are two kinds of people when it comes to asking for signs: unbelievers and believers. When the unbeliever asks for a sign, they want proof. The believer asks for a sign as confirmation. The Pharisees and Sadducees approached Jesus for a sign that would prove his identity. He said, "A wicked and adulterous generation looks for a sign, but none will be given it except the sign of Jonah" (Matt. 16:4). Proverbs 16:9 says, "The mind of man plans his way, but the Lord directs his steps" (NASB).

There is no end to the penchant of people to want to nail everything down; to make strategic plans and to hold fast to them. However, it is the Lord who directs our steps. Abraham's servant set a pretty high bar in this instance. It came to pass exactly as he asked, and yet he still sought discernment. Did you catch this last line?

Without saying a word, the man watched her closely to learn whether or not the LORD had made his journey successful.

In the final analysis, I see three things at constant interplay in our lives: the will of God; the plans of people; and our ever-changing circumstances. We ask for God's will to be done. We discern our plans as best we can to do the will of God. Stuff happens and we learn to trust God in the midst of it. The dynamic playing field of our lives with circumstances that change at least as quickly as the weather require vigilance and attunement to the Lord's ongoing guidance and direction. We often find ourselves in need of confirmation. The signs can seem silly and even absurd at times. Just know, God sees you, and his ability to guide you far exceeds your ability to read the signs. That said, don't be afraid or hesitant to ask for confirming signs.

People like Abraham's servant who say such things are themselves a sign to us.

The Prayer

Father, I don't want to be a person who constantly needs proof. I do acknowledge I regularly need confirming signs of your will and direction in my life. Show me how this works.

Give me the freedom to experiment in small ways that have less consequence so that when big things come along I will have a better sense of how your confirmations work. Mostly, I want to say I trust your will and I want to be the kind of person in whom you can trust my plans. And I want to be the kind of person who always trusts you in the ever-changing circumstances. Come, Holy Spirit, and train me to be such a person of faith. I pray in Jesus' name, amen.

The Questions

- How do you understand the interplay between God's will, our plans, and the ever-changing circumstances in our lives? How has the Lord worked to give you confirmations along the way?

. . . Don't Ask Why Me, but Why This? | 13

GENESIS 25:19–24 | This is the account of the family line of Abraham's son Isaac.

Abraham became the father of Isaac, and Isaac was forty years old when he married Rebekah daughter of Bethuel the Aramean from Paddan Aram and sister of Laban the Aramean.

Isaac prayed to the LORD on behalf of his wife, because she was childless. The LORD answered his prayer, and his wife Rebekah became pregnant. The babies jostled each other within her, and she said, "Why is this happening to me?" So she went to inquire of the Lord.

The Lord said to her,

"Two nations are in your womb,
   and two peoples from within you will be separated;
one people will be stronger than the other,
   and the older will serve the younger."

When the time came for her to give birth, there were twin boys in her womb.

Consider This

Observe the almost never-ending struggle in the life of a people pursuing the will of God. God promised more descendants than stars in the sky to childless Abraham and Sarah and waited until they were old to deliver their first son, Isaac. Isaac and Rebekah faced infertility and childlessness for twenty years and finally she became pregnant, then the struggle shifted to her womb. Remember, this was pre-ultrasound history. She didn't know she carried twins at the time—just that world war whatever was taking place in her belly.

The babies jostled each other within her, and she said, "Why is this happening to me?" So she went to inquire of the Lord.

People who say such things teach us another valuable lesson about the struggle of the life of faith. Here's her question: "Why is this happening to me?" Note: she didn't ask, "Why me?" That is the helpless question of a hapless bystander at best and a victim at worst. She asked, "Why this?" Rebekah, who tried for twenty years to have a child, accepted that life is struggle and difficulty. She was pressing in for the deeper question:

"Why is this happening to me?"

Now look at the next line: *So she went to inquire of the* Lord.

She wanted to know what the Lord was up to here. What might he be saying? How might he interpret this unusual struggle in her womb in the framework of his will? Was she worried she may lose the pregnancy? Maybe. Was she feeling anxious? Probably. She didn't know there was a mixed martial arts cage fight happening in her belly. She'd never been pregnant before. She sensed something was not right. Her response reveals how God's people deal with such anxious moments:

"Why is this happening to me?" So she went to inquire of the Lord.

People who say such things know the cosmic and eternal purposes of God get worked out in the chaotic everyday struggles of life. I do not mean to imply that there is some divine reason for every difficult or awful thing that happens in life. I don't subscribe to "there is a reason for everything" theology. I do, however, believe God speaks in specific ways and reveals particular things in the midst of our challenges, difficulties, and even tragedies. In other words, while everything that happens is not God's will, God has a will in everything that happens. It's why we want to learn this way of inquiring of the Lord in the happenings of our lives. It's why we say such things as this: *"Why is this happening to me?" So she went to inquire of the* L*ORD.*

God doesn't always respond so clearly, but he did here:

"Two nations are in your womb,

and two peoples from within you will be separated;

one people will be stronger than the other,

and the older will serve the younger."

While he didn't exactly say it was twins, he did offer a bit of a road map for the way ahead. Admittedly, this is all a bit extraordinary and even exceptional, and yet, something of the nature of the whole thing needs to normalize itself in our everyday lives. God is always saying things and doing things. He wants our participation in those things, which are indeed unfolding in the world around every single one of us. He wants us to pay attention to our everyday lives while discerning the work of the Word and the Spirit in the midst of them.

People who say such things come to understand the focus is not on *why* or *me*. The point is: What might you be saying and doing in *this*, Lord?

The Prayer

Father, I want to be a person who says such things. I don't want to be anxious about anything, but in everything I want to come before you with my inquiry, seeking out your Word and Spirit, your will and your ways. I know my life is not more important than anyone else's, and yet I know my life matters as much as anyone else's to you. I want to live that way in my life and through my relationships. Teach my spirit to abide in your Spirit. I renounce all victimhood in my life. Train my instincts not to ask: Why me? But, rather: Why this? Come, Holy Spirit, and train me to be such a person of faith. I pray in Jesus' name, amen.

The Questions

- Do you believe God wills and wants to speak into the specific situations and circumstances of your life? Are you learning to inquire of the Lord? Are you growing in your openness to the bigger story within which your own story unfolds and commingles?

. . . Show Us What Awakening Looks Like

14

GENESIS 28:16–22 | When Jacob awoke from his sleep, he thought, "Surely the LORD is in this place, and I was not aware of it." He was afraid and said, "How awesome is this place! This is none other than the house of God; this is the gate of heaven."

Early the next morning Jacob took the stone he had placed under his head and set it up as a pillar and poured oil on top of it. He called that place Bethel, though the city used to be called Luz.

Then Jacob made a vow, saying, "If God will be with me and will watch over me on this journey I am taking and will give me food to eat and clothes to wear so that I return safely to my father's household, then the LORD will be my God and this stone that I have set up as a pillar will be God's house, and of all that you give me I will give you a tenth."

Consider This

After some pretty dysfunctional parenting, followed by sibling rivalry, significant intrigue, deception, and even betrayal, we come to today's text. If you need to catch up with the plot line, start reading at Genesis 25:19.

Jacob was something of a hustler, if not a con artist, by this point. He had acquired his brother's birthright, and now through the intrigue of his mother and his willing compliance, he had managed to steal his older brother's blessing from Isaac. Jacob was a striver and a struggler. He always grasped for the advantage, fair or not. He wanted the edge. What this tells me is he wanted the goods without the God. He trusted himself, his will, and his ways rather than God's ways. Though he must be held responsible for his broken character, he can't be blamed. He came by it honestly.

We all do. No matter how blessed and beautiful our families may be, they are all broken. We all carry the cancer of sin and death in our souls, and we don't have to traverse far through our lineage to see where and how it metastasized through the generations (see Genesis 3). One generation fights a war and the next carries the wounds. Three generations later, the fear and anxiety surges, stealing peace while securing a broken prosperity. The feuds of rivalrous brothers and jealous sisters can carry on for years and poison the wells for generations to come. The only real difference in families is the accrued wealth with which they can conceal the fault lines of their broken bonds, run from their pain, and medicate their problems.

In the midst of such a twisted plot we learn a priceless truth from Jacob. As he ran into exile from his angry brother, Esau, he was found by God. History calls the story, "Jacob's Ladder."

> He had a dream in which he saw a stairway resting on the earth, with its top reaching to heaven, and the angels of God were ascending and descending on it. There above it stood the LORD, and he said: "I am the LORD, the God of your father Abraham and the God of Isaac. I will give you and your descendants the land on which you are lying." (Gen. 28:12–13)

Notice the stunning scope of the goodness and blessing of God, in spite of the brokenness of Jacob:

> "Your descendants will be like the dust of the earth, and you will spread out to the west and to the east, to the north and to the south. All peoples on earth will be blessed through you and your offspring. I am with you and will watch over you wherever you go, and I will bring you back to this land. I will not leave you until I have done what I have promised you." (Gen. 28:14–15)

This had nothing to do with the worthiness or worthlessness of Jacob (or Abraham and Isaac, for that matter) and everything to do with the willingness of God. I think my three favorite words in the Bible to this point come next: *When Jacob awoke . . .*

Now hear what he said: *"Surely the Lᴏʀᴅ is in this place, and I was not aware of it."*

People who say such things show us the greatest epiphany: through it all . . . God. He had always been there, through all the hiding and striving; through the messes of all the maneuvering to get ahead. The will and ways and working of God had never stopped. Angels ascending and descending, bringing "on earth as it is in heaven" (see Matthew 6:10) into the brokenness, through the brokenness, in spite of the brokenness, and maybe even because of the brokenness. And all of this because of the blessedness of this unlikely God.

He was afraid and said, "How awesome is this place! This is none other than the house of God; this is the gate of heaven."

People who say such things show us what awakening looks like.

The Prayer

Father, I want to be a person who says such things. I can be such a striver and a grasper. My own insecurities hold you at bay as I work so hard to hold it all together. In the process, my own brokenness unwittingly breaks those around me. Forgive me. Wake me up to this reality: "Surely the Lᴏʀᴅ is in this place, and I was not aware of it." Wake me up, Lord, and nothing I have lost will be lost any longer, and though it be nothing compared to the surpassing greatness of knowing your Son, Jesus, all I have gained will be yours. Come, Holy Spirit, and train me to be such a person of faith. I pray in Jesus' name, amen.

The Questions

- *"Surely the Lord is in this place, and I was not aware of it."* Have you experienced such an awakening in your life? Could it be unfolding now? Have you seen it in the lives others? Remember and reflect . . . and rejoice!

. . . Walk the Painful Path from Frustrated Desires to Core Longings Fulfilled

15

GENESIS 29:31–35 | When the Lord saw that Leah was not loved, he enabled her to conceive, but Rachel remained childless. Leah became pregnant and gave birth to a son. She named him Reuben, for she said, "It is because the Lord has seen my misery. Surely my husband will love me now."

She conceived again, and when she gave birth to a son she said, "Because the Lord heard that I am not loved, he gave me this one too." So she named him Simeon.

Again she conceived, and when she gave birth to a son she said, "Now at last my husband will become attached to me, because I have borne him three sons." So he was named Levi.

She conceived again, and when she gave birth to a son she said, "This time I will praise the Lord." So she named him Judah. Then she stopped having children.

Consider This

We come to a painful marriage story. It would behoove you to read the first thirty verses of Genesis 29. It is a whopper of a story and provides context for today's text.

In short, Jacob had two wives, Leah and Rachel—sister wives in the literal sense of the term. He was tricked into marrying Leah in order to get the one he truly loved, Rachel. It falls into the category of, "what comes around goes around." Jacob got a taste of his own medicine. Jacob did not love Leah, and she knew it.

Marriage has always been a mess. I find it helpful to revisit the curse issuing from the fall in the garden of Eden; particularly the curse upon the woman, which you will note extended into the marriage:

> To the woman he said,
>> "I will make your pains in childbearing very severe;
>> with painful labor you will give birth to children.
>> Your desire will be for your husband,
>> and he will rule over you." (Gen. 3:16)

We see the curse at play in today's text. Leah's desire was for her husband, and he ruled over her. Year's ago I learned a prescient saying that continues to instruct me in all relationships: "Who loves least has all the power." It's why most all relationships have power struggles, especially marriage. I understand Genesis 3:16b in an if-then frame, and I see it extending interchangeably between spouses. If your desire is for your spouse, your spouse will rule over you.

There is a lot of nuance here, so I will try to be clear. Surely it must be permissible to desire one's spouse. The issue is our core desire or longing. If our core longing is for our spouse, we are in for endless disappointment. The truth, whether we realize it or not, is that our core desire is for God alone. Only God can fulfill the core desire of our deepest heart. Our big problem comes when we seek to fulfill our core desire with someone or something other than God. Whoever or whatever we unwittingly turn into an idol, we turn to this person or thing to meet our core needs instead of God. We inevitably become a needy and unfulfilled person. This invariably makes us unattractive, no matter how outwardly appealing we may be. No matter how little or how much our partner tries to love us, we will feel insecure and unloved at the core. This is why there are so many loveless marriages all around us.

Leah did everything she possibly could to get Jacob to love her.

Leah became pregnant and gave birth to a son. She named him Reuben, for she said, "It is because the Lord has seen my misery. Surely my husband will love me now."

She conceived again, and when she gave birth to a son she said, "Because the Lord heard that I am not loved, he gave me this one too." So she named him Simeon.

Again she conceived, and when she gave birth to a son she said, "Now at last my husband will become attached to me, because I have borne him three sons." So he was named Levi.

How many couples over the years have turned to the solution of children to try and heal their broken marriage? It never works. Three kids later, and Leah still hadn't found the cure to her deeply broken heart. It came with the fourth child as her heart turned from her husband to her God.

She conceived again, and when she gave birth to a son she said, "This time I will praise the Lord." So she named him Judah. Then she stopped having children.

The solution is always found in turning to God, who alone can heal the broken hearts of a man and a woman, and only then can heal the marriage. Our disordered desires and longings, which give rise to so much of our brokenness as people, can only be healed and ordered by an abiding relationship with our Father, through the person of his Son, Jesus Christ, in the transforming power of the Holy Spirit.

"This time I will praise the Lord."

People who say such things show us what transformed desire looks like. After all the agony and pain of trying to satisfy her neediness through meeting the needs of another person, she finally turned to the Lord, and he healed her broken heart.

"This time I will praise the LORD."

Here's the beautiful part. At the end of Jacob's life, he instructed his sons with these words that he wanted to be buried at the family's burial site: "There Abraham and his wife Sarah were buried, there Isaac and his wife Rebekah were buried, and there I buried Leah" (Gen. 49:31).

Jacob buried Leah in the place of honor. By the mercy of God, she was transformed along the way from needy to lovely. In receiving the love of God, her heart was healed and readied to truly love and be loved by another person.

"This time I will praise the LORD."

She named the fourth child Judah, which means "praise." And we know who came from the tribe of Judah. We know him as the Lion of the tribe of Judah—Jesus Messiah.

People who say such things show us how our desperation, when brought to God, can lead to the fulfillment of our deepest desires.

The Prayer

Father, I want to be a person who says such things. I want my deepest desires to be fulfilled in you alone. Forgive me for the ways I repeatedly turn to other things and to other people to fulfill my desires. I confess so often my effort to meet the needs of others is merely a thin veil covering over my efforts to satisfy my own neediness. Teach me to bring my neediness to you. Train my heart to say, "This time I will praise the

Lord." Come, Holy Spirit, and train me to be such a person of faith. I pray in Jesus' name, amen.

The Questions

- Have you or are you experiencing loveless-ness in marriage? Do you know others who are experiencing this right now? Lift this word up over your marriage or that of another, "This time I will praise the Lord." Perhaps encourage them by sending them today's text.

16 . . . Show Us the Struggle Is Real

GENESIS 32:22–28 | That night Jacob got up and took his two wives, his two female servants and his eleven sons and crossed the ford of the Jabbok. After he had sent them across the stream, he sent over all his possessions. So Jacob was left alone, and a man wrestled with him till daybreak. When the man saw that he could not overpower him, he touched the socket of Jacob's hip so that his hip was wrenched as he wrestled with the man. Then the man said, "Let me go, for it is daybreak."

But Jacob replied, "I will not let you go unless you bless me."

The man asked him, "What is your name?"

"Jacob," he answered.

Then the man said, "Your name will no longer be Jacob, but Israel, because you have struggled with God and with humans and have overcome."

Consider This

Struggle.

It is a synonym for life. It means to wrestle, contend with, persevere, and even to agonize.

Jacob struggled. His mother experienced the struggle as he and Esau wrestled in her womb. Jacob came out of the womb grasping his brother's heel. He struggled to gain advantage over Esau the whole way through, trading for his birthright and deceiving for his blessing. He struggled to escape Esau's wrath. He struggled with Laban, his father-in-law, laboring for seven years to get the bride of his choice, Rachel, only to be deceived and get Leah instead. He struggled another seven years of hard labor to get Rachel. He struggled another six years, having his wages lowered ten times despite growing Laban's possessions. He struggled to escape Laban's hold on him. He escaped this stronghold only to learn of an immanent and inevitable confrontation with his brother, Esau. Now, on the eve of this dreadful date with Esau, Jacob finds himself in an epic struggle with God.

So Jacob was left alone, and a man wrestled with him till daybreak. When the man saw that he could not overpower him, he touched the socket of Jacob's hip so that his hip was wrenched as he wrestled with the man. Then the man said, "Let me go, for it is daybreak."

But Jacob replied, "I will not let you go unless you bless me."

People who say such things show us how struggle becomes blessing.

Then the man said, "Your name will no longer be Jacob, but Israel, because you have struggled with God and with humans and have overcome."

We all struggle. The big question we must all deal with is whether we will let go or not. How does a person let go? Most often it's not super intentional. They just kind of check out. With all the channels of entertainment available to us and the endless streams of social media, it is easy to become professionally distracted. Blaise Pascal said in his *Penses*, "We run heedlessly into the abyss, after putting something in front of us to stop us from seeing it."

Another way we let go is through anesthetizing ourselves to the pain of our struggles. The consumption of alcohol, which I don't see as a sin in and of itself, has arisen to the level of a sport with the burgeoning craft beer, bourbon, and wine industrial complex. Marijuana in every form under the sun is rolling like a wave, state by state, across the country. People are checking out en masse. We desperately want to escape the arduous struggle—and understandably so. Am I speaking to you? Because I know I am speaking to myself.

But Jacob replied, "I will not let you go unless you bless me."

My all-time favorite teacher, Oswald Chambers, wrote: "You must be willing to be placed on the altar and go through the fire; willing to experience what the altar represents—burning, purification, and separation for only one purpose—the elimination of every desire and affection not grounded in or directed toward God."* It resonates deeply with Leah's story, doesn't it?

A longtime close friend wrote me the other day, noting she had been praying for me and heard what she sensed was a word from the Lord for me. She risked sharing it with me, so I will risk sharing it with you.

> I don't want from him but for him. The pain is brutal— surgery with no anesthesia; no swig of whiskey, no bullet to bite—just searing, white-hot separation of marrow from bone, soul, and spirit—exposing. I actually know what I'm doing. The wholly holy unshakable will remain. No cancerous margins will remain. I am not closing the surgery until it's finished.

This resonated deeply with me in my own season of ongoing struggle. I risk sharing it because sometimes these kinds of words have a wider berth. My sense is it may be for others in my circle, including some who are reading. I risk sharing it also as an invitation for those who sense a burden to pray for me.

But Jacob replied, "I will not let you go unless you bless me."

To struggle with God and people is the norm, not the exception. Will we let go or hold on? There is always a blessing for those who will not let go.

---

* Oswald Chambers, ed. James Reimann, *My Utmost for His Highest* (Grand Rapids, MI: Discovery House, 2010), February 6.

Then the man said, "Your name will no longer be Jacob, but Israel, because you have struggled with God and with humans and have overcome."

And the blessing most often leaves a lasting scar, memorializing the struggle as a mark of glory. Jacob's blessing came with a limp. As the saying goes, be wary of trusting leaders who do not limp.

There's a fitting word from the apostle Paul with which we will close today:

> We are hard pressed on every side, but not crushed; perplexed, but not in despair; persecuted, but not abandoned; struck down, but not destroyed. We always carry around in our body the death of Jesus, so that the life of Jesus may also be revealed in our body. (2 Cor. 4:8–10)

But Jacob replied, "I will not let you go unless you bless me."
People who say such things show us that holding on to God is hard and yet is enough in the struggles of life. He will do the rest.

The Prayer

Father, I want to be a person who says such things. I come before you with my struggles—all of them. And yet I want to identify the deepest one of all: the struggle to hold on to you, to not let go. Your Spirit is willing, and yet I get tired and weary. I need more of you, Lord, and I know this means I must surrender more of me. Let the struggles in my life become the altar of your deeper work in my soul. Save me from thin distractions, from escaping into worthless things, from numbing my pain with my anesthesia of choice. I want the blessing, Jesus, which I know is you and all you bring. Come, Holy Spirit, and train me to be such a person of faith. I pray in Jesus' name, amen.

The Questions

- Have you learned to bring your struggle to God? Are you ready to let go or will you keep holding on until the blessing comes? Where is today's reading encouraging you? Challenging you?

. . . Show Us How to Build an Altar

17

GENESIS 35:1–3 | Then God said to Jacob, "Go up to Bethel and settle there, and build an altar there to God, who appeared to you when you were fleeing from your brother Esau."

So Jacob said to his household and to all who were with him, "Get rid of the foreign gods you have with you, and purify yourselves and change your clothes. Then come, let us go up to Bethel, where I will build an altar to God, who answered me in the day of my distress and who has been with me wherever I have gone."

63

Consider This

When is the last time you built an altar?

We will say goodbye to Jacob today but not before he completes the God cycle. What is the God cycle? Thanks for asking. It is the movement from promise to struggle to blessing to worship. Remember, it was at Bethel where God first revealed himself to Jacob through a dream. As Jacob ran from the consequences of his broken life, God met him in a dream, revealing to him the covenant promise that was given to Abraham and Isaac would also determine his destiny.

Perhaps the biggest lesson of the Bible so far is how the promises of God necessarily mean struggle. Something in us wants to believe the presence and promises of God mean an easier path. It does not. God's promises mean an infinitely and eternally better life, but they almost guarantee a harder path. The way of the cross is the way of blessing and yet struggle.

After the promising dream in Bethel, the next twenty years delivered the struggle for Rachel, the struggle of Leah, the onerous yoke of Laban, and more than a dozen children who would define the legacy—and all of this under the impending cloud of doom from an angry older brother bent on revenge.

Remember, through it all . . . God. Promise. Struggle. Blessing. God blessed Jacob. God prospered Jacob. God favored Jacob. God delivered Jacob. Following the miraculous change of heart of older brother, Esau, and the happy reunion on the far side of the River Jabbok, God instructed Jacob to complete the cycle. The time had come to worship.

Then God said to Jacob, "Go up to Bethel and settle there, and build an altar there to God, who appeared to you when you were fleeing from your brother Esau."

Promise. Struggle. Blessing. Worship. Certainly we worship our way through it all, and yet, there is something to be said for building a new altar from time to time to mark significant God-moments and faith milestones. They call for something more than the usual.

So Jacob said to his household and to all who were with him, "Get rid of the foreign gods you have with you, and purify yourselves and change your clothes. Then come, let us go up to Bethel, where I will build an altar to God, who answered me in the day of my distress and who has been with me wherever I have gone."

People who say such things show us what building an altar requires. First, it's a community affair: *"So Jacob said to his household and to all who were with him . . ."* Second, it means a personal and community call to repentance: *"Get rid of the foreign gods you have with you."* Third, it means a call to a renewed heart-level consecration to God: *"Purify yourselves."* Fourth, it calls for an outward sign of the inward reality: *"Change your clothes."* Finally, it means sharing the testimony that it might become the shared witness of all: *"Then come, let us go up to Bethel, where I will build an altar to God, who answered me in the day of my distress and who has been with me wherever I have gone."*

Altars powerfully mark the movements of God while extending them forward for all who will kneel. So let me ask you again: When is the last time you built an altar? It's been too long for me. I see one coming on the horizon.

The Prayer

Father, I want to be a person who says such things. Help me become this kind of person in my deep heart and this kind of leader in my relationships with others. You don't so much need this from me as you want it for me. Guide me in the who, what, where, when, and how of building an altar to mark your movement in my life, to complete the cycle of promise, struggle, and blessing with worship. Come, Holy Spirit, and train me to be such a person of faith. I pray in Jesus' name, amen.

The Questions

- So when is the last time you built an altar? What was that like? How did it go? What might the altar on the horizon look like in your life, family, church, community?

18 . . . Lean into the Long Game of Redemption

GENESIS 50:19–20 | But Joseph said to them, "Don't be afraid. Am I in the place of God? You intended to harm me, but God intended it for good to accomplish what is now being done, the saving of many lives."

Consider This

There is one thing Joseph said which captures the whole of Genesis, this first masterwork of Scripture.

But Joseph said to them, "Don't be afraid. Am I in the place of God? You intended to harm me, but God intended it for good to accomplish what is now being done, the saving of many lives."

It's a complex story, to put it mildly, and too much to unpack here, but Joseph's brothers sold him into slavery, setting his life on a path of unmitigated suffering and struggle and yet unparalleled favor and fortune. Today's text comes at the end of the story as Joseph stood before his brothers as the second in command to Pharaoh himself. He stood before the ones whose cruelty and treacherous betrayal caused him unmentionable trauma and endless loss. The tables had turned and they stood before him in need of what he alone could provide: food in the face of a destroying famine. He stood before them with absolute power. He could have thrown them all into prison and left their family to starve. Instead, he showed them absolute mercy.

But Joseph said to them, "Don't be afraid. Am I in the place of God? You intended to harm me, but God intended it for good to accomplish what is now being done, the saving of many lives."

Where was Joseph's bitterness? His anger? His revenge? He did not excuse what they did or their intentions. He forgave them. It seems he had forgiven them long ago. This was a moment of profound reconciliation and, even more, a celebration of redemption.

You intended to harm me, but God intended it for good to accomplish what is now being done, the saving of many lives.

People who say such things know in their deepest guts this simple truth: What God allows, he redeems. Abraham and Sarah knew it. Isaac and Rebekah knew it. Jacob and Rachel and Leah knew it. Even more, Esau knew it as did Joseph. Life can be difficult, unfair, and unmercifully cruel. Bad things happen to good people, while good things happen to bad people. There is no understanding it or hope to make sense of it in any semblance of the short run. Because God plays the long game, redemption takes the long view. And redemption requires our participation. It can take years to work through the bitterness, the unforgiveness, and the often unquenchable thirst for revenge—and this in the best of people. What God allows, he redeems. It can take decades, lifetimes, even generations for redemption to run its course.

Did you catch the secret to participating in redemption—besides working through your bitterness, unforgiveness, anger, victim complex, and revenge fantasies? It was right there in the text:

But Joseph said to them, "Don't be afraid. Am I in the place of God?"

Joseph knew he was not in the place of God. He knew his place, and he knew God's place, and he kept them sorted. He seemed to know full well that God redeems what he allows, which meant leaning into redemption instead of revenge. From the bottom of a well to the shackles of a slave to the dungeon of a king and back again, Joseph knew redemption must begin with him. As hard as it seems sometimes, this is always within our reach. Nowhere do we see it more clearly than in our dear Lord Jesus.

The nineteenth-century Danish theologian and philosopher Søren Kierkegaard captured in words what every saint before and since have known in their lives: "Life must be lived forward, but it can only be understood backward."

May we aspire to become people who say such things with our lips and our lives.

The Prayer

Father, I want to be a person who says such things. You are God, and I am not. Though I am in the miry, muddy middle of it all, you see the end from the beginning. Help me know you are at work to take what was intended for bad and turn it to good; that you are, in fact, working all things together for my good. Train my spirit to forgive. Draw out the bitterness in my heart. Heal my anger and empower me to trade in my sense of revenge for your redemption. Come, Holy Spirit, and train me to be such a person of faith. I pray in Jesus' name, amen.

The Questions

- Do you have or know of a story where God worked something out intended for bad into something good? How are you doing with your own stored-up bitterness, unforgiveness, anger, and revenge fantasies? Are you ready to let them go? Are you ready to step out of the place of God?

19 ... Yearn for the Living God

PSALM 84:1–4 | How lovely is your dwelling place,
 LORD Almighty!
My soul yearns, even faints,
 for the courts of the LORD;
my heart and my flesh cry out
 for the living God.
Even the sparrow has found a home,
 and the swallow a nest for herself,
 where she may have her young—
a place near your altar,
 LORD Almighty, my King and my God.
Blessed are those who dwell in your house;
 they are ever praising you.

Consider This

As we close out Genesis, the book of origins and biblical backstory, it will be good to pause and make camp for a few days of remembrance, reflection, and worship. This is what the Psalms do in and for us. For the next few days we will slowly walk our way through Psalm 84, a psalm for the awakened—those who have left behind the conventions of predictable, domesticated religion and abandoned themselves to the goodness and mercy of God. People who say such things as the words of Psalm 84 have set their heart "on pilgrimage" (v. 5). They have, in the famous words about by Elvis Presley, "left the building."

How lovely is your dwelling place,
Lord Almighty!

Speaking of leaving the building, we have become accustomed to think of this "dwelling place" as a building, a particular place one goes to worship. To be fair, the psalmist does reference the temple here, however the temple is itself a sign pointing to something far greater. Remember the banner text lifted up over this entire series:

> People who say such things show that they are looking for a country of their own. If they had been thinking of the country they had left, they would have had opportunity to return. Instead, they were longing for a better country—a heavenly one. Therefore God is not ashamed to be called their God, for he has prepared a city for them. (Heb. 11:14–16).

With the people of God, the roots didn't grow downward, they grew upward. Herein lies the chief advantage of the tabernacle over the temple. The tabernacle embodied the movement of God's people. It was portable, defining the center of the community and yet moving with the community. Something about a permanent place centers the gravity in the place rather than in God. Something about us struggles with movement. We want it and yet we also want to "put down roots," as the saying goes.

The story of Genesis reveals a God who moves and who longs for his people to move with him.

> My soul yearns, even faints,
>   for the courts of the LORD;
> my heart and my flesh cry out
>   for the living God.

People who say such things show us that going to the so-called place of God can never be a substitute for seeking the face of God. We must come to tangibly grasp that the courts of the Lord are everywhere, all around us, all the time, and always open. In another psalm, the psalmist speaks of entering the gates of the Lord "with thanksgiving and his courts with praise" (Ps. 100:4a). What is the sign that we have left the building of a comfortable, domesticated faith (which is not really faith at all)? Our heart and flesh cry out for the living God. The more of God we know, the more of God we long for. We long for a better country—a heavenly one. The question is not: Are you longing for heaven? But, rather: Are you longing for a better country?

Perhaps the twin harbingers of a domesticated faith (which is hardly faith at all) are these: a temple mind-set and a heaven mentality. We want to settle down into a comfortable life of being blessed by God instead of struggling with God for the coming of his kingdom, and we primarily think of heaven as the place we go when we die. This is the Christian faith harnessed to the American dream: a comfortable life now and eternal comfort after that.

So how might we contrast the awakened life to this domesticated faith? Instead of a temple mind-set, awakened faith holds a tabernacle mentality—ever moving with a God on the move. Instead of a heaven mentality, the awakened soul holds to an "on earth as it is in heaven" mind-set (see Matthew 6:10). This is the Christian faith harnessed to the kingdom vision: eternal life now, in the presence and power of God, in the faith-filled struggle of laboring for "on earth as it is in heaven," and a seamless crossing over at our death, ascending into the heavens, where we take a prime seat in the balcony of the communion of saints until the kingdom comes in final glory.

The questions we must grapple with are these: Do we want a captivating faith or will we settle for a faith in captivity? Do I long for an arresting demonstration of the Spirit of God in my life or will I succumb to arrested development of my soul?

When Scripture says, "The Word became flesh and made his dwelling among us" (John 1:14), it uses the language of "tabernacling." The presence and power of God tabernacled in Jesus of Nazareth, and he wills to do the same through his Spirit in his people, the body of Christ. We are the dwelling place of God. And there is infinite room for more to come inside. Even the whole creation.

Even the sparrow has found a home,
and the swallow a nest for herself,
where she may have her young—
a place near your altar,
LORD Almighty, my King and my God.

People who say such things know they have already arrived and yet are still on the way, ever making room for more. And though the journey may get harder, it will also keep getting better.

Blessed are those who dwell in your house;
    they are ever praising you.

The Prayer

Father, I want to be a person who says such things. My heart and flesh cry out for you, the living God. Clarify my vision and shift my mentality and mind-set. Shake me from my comfortable slumber. At least bring me to the consciousness that would require me to choose it over a life of awakened faith. I am so weary of the lazy, mediocre way of life that some want to call faith. I want the real thing and I will settle for nothing less. I want Jesus. Yes, Lord, my heart and flesh cry out for you. Come, Holy Spirit, and train me to be such a person of faith. I pray in Jesus' name, amen.

The Questions

• How do you relate to this contrast outlined in today's reading between domesticated religion and awakened faith? Between a captivating life and a life in captivity? Can you honestly say this: "My soul yearns for the living God"? Do you want to be able to say it honestly?

20 . . . Set Their Hearts on Pilgrimage

PSALM 84:5 | Blessed are those whose strength is in you, whose hearts are set on pilgrimage.

Consider This

This, people, is what we want to say:

Blessed are those whose strength is in you,

whose hearts are set on pilgrimage.

People who say such things have left the building, joined the movement, and they aren't turning back. In the end, there are two kinds of people in life: pilgrims and tourists. Tourists take vacations to escape their predictable and often monotonous lives. Don't hear me wrong. Vacations aren't the problem. Pilgrims take vacations too. The difference? The minute one vacation is over, the tourist starts planning and living for the next one. Pilgrims need R & R ("rest and relaxation," for you readers in the majority world who aren't familiar with our American ways). Tourists live for it.

Blessed are those whose strength is in you,

whose hearts are set on pilgrimage.

The tourist is always looking for the next experience. Will it be Disney World or a river cruise? The pilgrim ever prepares for the next assignment. Will it be reaching out to a young couple whose marriage is in trouble or helping a homeless family get a roof over their heads? The tourist tends to categorize life into family, work, and leisure. The Christian tourist adds a fourth category: faith—which gets translated into church. The pilgrim moves seamlessly between family, work, and leisure. Church ceased to be a category somewhere along the way, stopped being a place, and became translated into faith.

The tourist turns to God when in trouble, trial, or hardship. They need God to give them strength. Faith is a resource when other resources fail. The pilgrim is a faith-filled seeker in all things and at all times. Their strength is in God: Father, Son, and Holy Spirit. Their heart is set on pilgrimage. God doesn't so much give them strength; God is their strength.

The tourist is ever exploring the sites and stories of history, watching someone else's big game, and escaping into the next experience. The pilgrim is making history; albeit quietly and most often unknowingly. The pilgrim is on the playing field, losing their way into the win and ever engaging God in every experience of life. Remember, pilgrimage isn't the occasional religious trip to the holy land. It is the lifelong journey of the heart.

What are you saying today, Lord? What are you doing today, Lord? How do you want to move in my life today, Lord? What are you up to in my family, Lord? What might you be doing in the house across the street, Lord?

Blessed are those whose strength is in you,

whose hearts are set on pilgrimage.

So don't go canceling your next trip to the Bahamas (though they could use your help down in the Abacos, for sure). People who say such things set their hearts on pilgrimage.

The Prayer

Father, I want to be a person who says such things. I want to be on pilgrimage. I want to set my heart on pilgrimage. My strength is in you. Yes, Lord, you are my strength. Come, Holy Spirit, and train me to be such a person of faith. I pray in Jesus' name, amen.

The Questions

- So how about it? Tourist or pilgrim? Does the contrast help you?

. . . Learn to Embrace the Valley of Vision

21

PSALM 84:6–7 | As they pass through the Valley of Baka,
   they make it a place of springs;
   the autumn rains also cover it with pools.
They go from strength to strength,
   till each appears before God in Zion.

Consider This

The Valley of Baka is a place where physical terrain becomes spiritual geography. Historians believe it refers to an arid valley near Jerusalem where a certain kind of weeping tree (perhaps a balsam tree) grew. The word *Baka* means "to weep."

No matter who you are, young or old, wealthy or poor, times of sadness are bound to come. They come with losses, disappointments, failures, and sometimes even successes. Often they can protract themselves into seasons of depression. At times, a path of depression can lead a person off the pilgrim's trail and into outright despair. If this describes you, you must reach out for help.

The more one reads, hears, and prays the Psalms, the more they realize the Valley of Baka cannot be avoided. It must be experienced, engaged, and passed through. We must not run from or try to escape our sorrows. Learning to welcome the emotion of sadness can be a difficult lesson for the soul, especially in a land where the core value is the "pursuit of happiness" (which meant something quite different to the ones who wrote those words in the Declaration of Independence than it does in the present day).

There is the sadness common to life and then there is the sorrow of God. Despite all the joy we perceive in him, Scripture refers to Jesus as "a man of sorrows" (Isa. 53:3 NASB). Scripture also describes him as the pioneer pilgrim of faith. To follow him means at times we, too, will perhaps experience more sorrow and sadness than the average person. Jesus spent his life in the gap between the blessedness of God and the brokenness of the world. The more we truly enter into the brokenness of others, sharing their burden, the more we will take on and help carry their sorrow. In other words, the closer we grow to God, the more God will entrust us to share in his sorrow for this broken world.

It is easy to be angry at the world. Angry prophets are a dime a dozen. It's another thing altogether to allow our own brokenness to be transformed in the furnace of the valley for the sake of others. This is the essence of pilgrimage. Now watch what happens when this happens:

As they pass through the Valley of Baka,
they make it a place of springs;

Wherever we embrace the brokenness of Jesus—first in our own valleys and then for the sake of others—the Father pours out the living water of the Spirit. The Valley of Weeping becomes a place of springs. There is a mysterious passage in Paul's second letter to the Corinthian church that seems instructive. I have wrestled with it many times:

> We always carry around in our body the death of Jesus, so that the life of Jesus may also be revealed in our body. For we who are alive are always being given over to death for Jesus' sake, so that his life may also be revealed in our mortal body. So then, death is at work in us, but life is at work in you. (2 Cor. 4:10–12)

This is a text to sit down with, sink into, and say, "Come, Holy Spirit, and instruct and interpret this text to me in my own life." It is a pilgrimage text, and here's the beautiful bonus of a heart set on pilgrimage:

They go from strength to strength,

till each appears before God in Zion.

For the one whose heart is set on pilgrimage, the Valley of Baka is the place of profound growth. The deeper the valley, the deeper the potential for transformation. We love the mountain tops and, indeed, the Lord meets us there, but he does his best work in us in the valley. Let's give Paul the last word—again from 2 Corinthians:

> Therefore we do not lose heart. Though outwardly we are wasting away, yet inwardly we are being renewed

day by day. For our light and momentary troubles are achieving for us an eternal glory that far outweighs them all. So we fix our eyes not on what is seen, but on what is unseen, since what is seen is temporary, but what is unseen is eternal. (4:16–18)

The Prayer

For the prayer today I will share one of my favorite prayers. It is called The Valley of Vision and comes from a book by the same title that is a collection of Puritan prayers.

Lord, high and holy, meek and lowly,
Thou hast brought me to the valley of vision,
where I live in the depths but see thee in the heights;
*   hemmed in by mountains of sin I behold thy glory.*
Let me learn by paradox
that the way down is the way up,
that to be low is to be high,
that the broken heart is the healed heart, that the contrite
*   spirit is the rejoicing spirit, that the repenting soul is the*
*   victorious soul, that to have nothing is to possess all,*
that to bear the cross is to wear the crown, that to give
*   is to receive,*
that the valley is the place of vision.
Lord, in the daytime stars can be seen from deepest wells,
*   and the deeper the wells the brighter thy stars shine;*
Let me find thy light in my darkness, thy life in my death,
thy joy in my sorrow, thy grace in my sin,
thy riches in my poverty thy glory in my valley.

Father, I want to be a person who says such things. Come, Holy Spirit, and train me to be such a person of faith. I pray in Jesus' name, amen.

The Questions

· What has been your experience in the Valley of Baka? Are you struggling there now to find the place of springs? Are you feeling alone in it?

. . . Don't Have Priorities, They Have a Priority — 22

PSALM 84:8–12 | Hear my prayer, Lord God Almighty;
  listen to me, God of Jacob.
Look on our shield, O God;
  look with favor on your anointed one.

Better is one day in your courts
  than a thousand elsewhere;
I would rather be a doorkeeper in the house of my God
  than dwell in the tents of the wicked.
For the Lord God is a sun and shield;
  the Lord bestows favor and honor;
no good thing does he withhold
  from those whose walk is blameless.

Lord Almighty,
  blessed is the one who trusts in you.

Consider This

When I was a kid I remember asking my grandfather (a.k.a. "Peepaw") one day to tell me his favorite Bible verse. Without hesitating, he said:

I would rather be a doorkeeper in the house of my God
than dwell in the tents of the wicked.

My first job in the church was doorkeeper.

It happened like clockwork, every Sunday morning at the First United Methodist Church of Dumas, Arkansas. As the service came to a close and the choir prepared to file out of the choir loft, I would ease to the edge of my front row seat. As the organist struck the first chord of the postlude, I launched like a lion bounding toward the door through which they would exit. I eagerly swung the large oaken door and held it open, beaming with pride as the grateful choir passed through.

I would rather be a doorkeeper in the house of my God
than dwell in the tents of the wicked.

My second job in the church was doorkeeper.

It happened like clockwork, every single night at the Central United Methodist Church in Fayetteville, Arkansas. As the last cars cleared the parking lot of the large church campus, I would set my law books aside, grab my keys, and make the rounds, shaking all the doors and making sure the alarms were set. Yes, I was the security guard.

I would rather be a doorkeeper in the house of my God
than dwell in the tents of the wicked.

Jesus said it like this, "What good will it be for someone to gain the whole world, yet forfeit their soul? Or what can anyone give in exchange for their soul?" (Matt. 16:26).

People who say such things don't have priorities; they have a priority. When you think about it, isn't it a little bit absurd to have priorities? I mean, isn't the whole point of priority to be about one thing? Doesn't making the word plural destroy the word and any meaning it could ever hope to have? Ponder that with me. There can only be one first, right?

I would rather be a doorkeeper in the house of my God
than dwell in the tents of the wicked.

I would rather be nothing with Jesus than something without him. Why? Because to be something without Jesus is nothing, and to be nothing with Jesus is still everything.

Lord Almighty,
blessed is the one who trusts in you.

The Prayer

Father, I want to be a person who says such things. "I would rather be a doorkeeper in the house of my God than to dwell in the tents of the wicked." I would rather be nothing with you, Jesus, than to try to be something without you. Clarify my aspirations and intentions and give me an undivided heart, that I might worthily magnify your holy name. Come, Holy Spirit, and train me to be such a person of faith. I pray in Jesus' name, amen.

The Questions

- What would it take to bring your priorities down to a priority? What would it be? And by the way, do you have a doorkeeper in the house of the Lord story?

23 . . . Know God Is Enough

PSALM 23 | The LORD is my shepherd, I lack nothing.
He makes me lie down in green pastures,
he leads me beside quiet waters,
he refreshes my soul.
He guides me along the right paths
for his name's sake.
Even though I walk
through the darkest valley,
I will fear no evil,
for you are with me;
your rod and your staff,
they comfort me.

You prepare a table before me
in the presence of my enemies.
You anoint my head with oil;
my cup overflows.
Surely your goodness and love will follow me
all the days of my life,
and I will dwell in the house of the LORD
forever.

Consider This

Did you just do a flyover? You know what I mean. Did you just hit auto-pilot when you saw the famed Twenty-Third Psalm, consider that you knew it, and skip down to this part of the entry? If so, go back and read it again—out loud, and this time with feeling.

Psalm 23 is one of those texts that can become so familiar that we don't even see it any more. It gets relegated to funerals, and for most churchgoing people, that's how they know it. It is the standard bearer of funerals; likely because of that bit in there about the valley of the shadow of death.

Despite the folder it gets filed in, Psalm 23 is one of the most comprehensive, profound, and prolific texts in all of Scripture. It stunningly captures the nature of a lifelong, personal, pilgrimage walk with God. If Psalm 84 is the view of the pilgrim way from the outside looking in, Psalm 23 is the view from the inside out. Over the next six days we will walk our way through the green pastures, still waters, right paths, valley of death, enemy defying, goodness- and mercy-chasing masterwork of poetic prayer. We will repeat the whole chapter each day, bringing our focus to one of the six verses. You already know I will challenge you to read aloud to hear, ruminate, "rememberize," research, and rehearse the text. Before we are done, this will become far more than a death text; it will be a life text.

The LORD is my shepherd, I lack nothing.

People who say such things, and really mean them, know the most important truth in life.

The LORD is . . .

The Lord, the God of heaven and earth, Father, Son, and Holy Spirit, the Ancient of Days, the Lion of Judah, the Creator, Redeemer, and Sustainer of all that was and is and ever shall be; this God is, period. But it's not enough to leave it there.

The Lord is my . . .

This God is my Shepherd. My Shepherd. Mine. And yours. Not ours just yet, because there is no "ours" without their first being a "mine" and a "yours." I am pretty adamant about the second person plural "you" of the Bible; that the relationship with God is personal, but never individual. I want to be crystal clear on this matter of pronouns though. There is no second-person plural without first-person singular. Unless this God is my God, to say he is "our" God rings hollow as a meaningless claim. But it's not enough to leave it there.

The Lord is my shepherd . . .

This claim—my Shepherd—translates every doctrine, every creed, every canon, and every orthodox formulation and theological framework ever recorded concerning the Christian faith and brings it into the fold of personal relationship. Not us. Not we. But me, myself, and I—personal, attached, bonded. But it's not enough to leave it there.

The Lord is my shepherd, I lack nothing.

This Shepherd knows me, the real me, the true me, the one behind every lie, the me behind every shaded truth of my true identity, the me behind every need to appear better than I am, every falsehood, mask, unholy attachment, misspent longing, craving for control, and striving manipulation to make my own way, fulfill my own desires, meet my own needs, satisfy my own ambitions, be better than everybody else, and build my own kingdom. But it's not enough to leave it there.

This Shepherd who knows me—the good and true, the bad and ugly—this Shepherd loves me, wants the best for me, wills to shape my desires and then to fulfill them; delights in me, rejoices, yes, even sings over me. He loves me especially, extravagantly, and eternally.

The Lord is my shepherd, I lack nothing.

This is everything. And because this is everything, I lack nothing.

People who say such things, and increasingly mean them, know the most important truth in life: God is enough.

Everything in him is mine. And everything is mine in him.

Everything in me is his. And everything is his in me.

The Lord is my shepherd, I lack nothing.

The Prayer

Father, I want to be a person who says such things. It is not enough to know about you and even who you are. I want to know you close, as my Shepherd. I want to know your voice and trust you heart and obey your whisper. Open my mind and heart this week to draw near to you; maybe like never before. Come, Holy Spirit, and train me to be such a person of faith. I pray in Jesus' name, amen.

The Questions

- What has been your experience with Psalm 23? Is it part of your life or the occasional funeral remembrance? Do you relate to God as Shepherd?

24 . . . Lack Nothing

PSALM 23 | The Lord is my shepherd, I lack nothing.
    He makes me lie down in green pastures,
  he leads me beside quiet waters,
    he refreshes my soul.
  He guides me along the right paths
    for his name's sake.
  Even though I walk
    through the darkest valley,
  I will fear no evil,
    for you are with me;
  your rod and your staff,
    they comfort me.

  You prepare a table before me
    in the presence of my enemies.
  You anoint my head with oil;
    my cup overflows.
  Surely your goodness and love will follow me
    all the days of my life,
  and I will dwell in the house of the Lord
  forever.

Consider This

Sometimes the poetry gets in the way of the point.

As I have begun working through this NIV translation of the psalm, I find myself chafing against it a bit. I am so used to the funeral version, which would be the King James Version, and all its finely poetic Elizabethan English. The opening line is grooved in my soul like a well-worn path: "The LORD is my shepherd; I shall not want." Hence, my opening statement.

"I lack nothing" says everything about my reality if the Lord is my Shepherd. "I shall not want" says something about my behavior if the Lord is my Shepherd. See the difference here? The Hebrew text, in my limited understanding of it, seems to favor the more recent NIV translation: "I lack nothing." To say, "I have a good Shepherd, therefore I lack nothing," is quite a different thing than to say, "I have a good Shepherd, therefore I should not want anything." We could spend a week of discipleship right here, but we must press on. In lieu of that, I want to ask you to repeat those eight words out loud—*The LORD is my shepherd, I lack nothing*—for the next minute. It will have impact.

The LORD is my shepherd, I lack nothing.

Now, besides the problem of the glaring comma splice, we are good—on to the text of the day.

He makes me lie down in green pastures,
he leads me beside quiet waters,
he refreshes my soul.

There is a great difference between, "The LORD is my shepherd," and the more common bumper-sticker sentiment, "Jesus is my copilot." I am not the pilot of my own ship. Nor am I the copilot. I do not need someone to help me when I am in a pinch. I need constant guidance, provision, care, and direction. I am a sheep. Jesus is the Shepherd. He knows what I need, and he supplies it. Green pastures for grazing and later for stretching out and resting in when I'm full? Check! Still waters to drink from with their serenity in the midst of anxiety? Check! Those are not goods and services the Shepherd provides, they are the fruit of his presence. They come with the Shepherd.

I still mostly live with a "God, help me!" mentality. And I need a lot of help. I need help with my kids. I need help with my job. I need help with making ends meet. I need help with my diet and exercise. I need help with my sadness. I need help with my insecurities. You get the point.

I am growing and want to grow more in a "God, have me!" mind-set. If the Lord is my Shepherd, he has me. *And I lack nothing.* Green pastures? Check! Still waters? Check! I don't need to worry about all my needs.

The Lord is my shepherd, I lack nothing.

I need only learn to live in an abiding relationship with the Shepherd; listening and hearing, watching and waiting, receiving and giving.

The Lord is my shepherd, I lack nothing.

This is not a statement of intention. It is a declaration of faith. It doesn't say he will help me find green pastures and he will help me locate still waters or he will help me do a better job with my soul care. Help me. Help me. Help me. It's transactional faith. It's good faith, but it is not goal faith.

"Have me." That is transcendent faith. This is the stuff of the deep transition we are into now. The shift is from how God helps me to who God is to me. The shift is from God is my copilot, on standby to help as needed, to: *The Lord is my shepherd, I lack nothing.*

People who say such things are making the shift. They increasingly find their soul restored not so much by the green pastures and the still waters but by the presence of God himself. And they are becoming bold, confident, not anxious, and unafraid.

The Prayer

Father, I want to be a person who says such things. I feel like I need so much help, and you are so faithful to help me. I want to make the deep shift from "Help me!" prayers to a "Have me!" life. I need you to help me with this. And there I go again. You are my Shepherd. I lack nothing. Yes, Lord, with you I lack nothing. Have me. Come, Holy Spirit, and train me to be such a person of faith. I pray in Jesus' name, amen.

The Questions

- Are you grasping this challenge to shift from "Help me!" to "Have me!" faith? What might this mean for you?

. . . Know How to Receive Guidance from the Shepherd

25

PSALM 23 | The LORD is my shepherd, I lack nothing.
  He makes me lie down in green pastures,
he leads me beside quiet waters,
  he refreshes my soul.
He guides me along the right paths

for his name's sake.
Even though I walk
   through the darkest valley,
I will fear no evil,
   for you are with me;
your rod and your staff,
   they comfort me.

You prepare a table before me
   in the presence of my enemies.
You anoint my head with oil;
   my cup overflows.
Surely your goodness and love will follow me
   all the days of my life,
and I will dwell in the house of the Lord
forever.

Consider This

He guides me along the right paths
   for his name's sake.

There's an old story about a tour group in the Holy Land you may have heard. After hearing a teaching on the Twenty-Third Psalm and how the shepherd always goes ahead of the sheep to lead, guide, and protect them, they went out to the country-side in search of such a demonstration. The guide sent them to a familiar pasture where they noticed a flock of frazzled sheep coming over the hillside with no shepherd out in front. Instead, the shepherd came behind the flock. A bit bewildered, one of the women approached the shepherd and asked him about the apparently suspect teaching they had just received. He replied, "Oh, no. I am not the shepherd. I am the butcher!"

It reminds me of one of the most oft-cited and proof-texted Scripture verses in the Bible: "The thief comes only to steal and kill and destroy; I have come that they may have life, and have it to the full" (John 10:10).

It should be noted that this text comes from the larger passage where Jesus speaks of himself as both the Gate for the sheep and the Good Shepherd.

> "The gatekeeper opens the gate for him, and the sheep listen to his voice. He calls his own sheep by name and leads them out. When he has brought out all his own, he goes on ahead of them, and his sheep follow him because they know his voice. But they will never follow a stranger; in fact, they will run away from him because they do not recognize a stranger's voice." (John 10:3–5)

> "I am the good shepherd; I know my sheep and my sheep know me—just as the Father knows me and I know the Father—and I lay down my life for the sheep." (John 10:14–15)

Now consider today's text in that light:
He guides me along the right paths
  for his name's sake.

We follow Jesus. He leads us. He speaks. We listen. It can seem so ethereal and nebulous and inaccessible. How do we know the voice in our head from the voice of Jesus? Let me suggest a three-step process whereby we grow in perceiving and pursuing the guidance of the Good Shepherd along the right paths: Inspiration. Imitation. Impartation.

Inspiration comes from the inspired text—the Bible. We must keep these inspired texts before us, ever in the foreground of our vision. Matthew, Mark, Luke, and John are the premier guides for discipleship. I am convicted as I write of my own present lack of immersion in these miraculous Gospel accounts. Am I paying attention to these ancient texts and being inspired by the whole story at ever-increasing levels of detail?

Imitation comes from inspiration. It means doing the kinds of things Jesus does in the Gospels. It means obeying his teaching and imaginatively putting into practice his words and deeds. When Jesus tells Martha she is anxious about many things, but only one thing is necessary and Mary has found it by sitting at his feet (see Luke 10:38–42), am I engaging this text at the level of practice in my own life? Am I practicing the story?

Impartation comes as the fruit of inspiration and imitation. If inspiration and imitation are practice, impartation is playing the game itself. It is improvisational. We know the kinds of things Jesus did. We have practiced them. By the power of the Spirit, we have his mind. Now he can impart guidance to us along right paths for his name's sake. By the power of the Word and Spirit, he is "in" us and we are "in" him. We learn to "run in the path of [his] commands," as the psalmist put it (119:32).

He guides me along the right paths
  for his name's sake.

People who say such things are learning to live freely and lightly, improvising along the path as the Shepherd guides.

The Prayer

Father, I want to be a person who says such things. Bring me into direct discipleship with you. Let inspiration become imitation become impartation. I am weary of more and more information that doesn't take me anywhere. And I'm weary of just trying to behave myself. I want to become like you, Jesus. Impart your mind, heart, will, and ways to me. Come, Holy Spirit, and train me to be such a person of faith. I pray in Jesus' name, amen.

The Question

- How might inspiration, imitation, and impartation become a growing and flourishing movement in your life?

. . . Fear No Evil

26

PSALM 23 | The Lord is my shepherd, I lack nothing.
  He makes me lie down in green pastures,
he leads me beside quiet waters,
  he refreshes my soul.
He guides me along the right paths
  for his name's sake.

Even though I walk
   through the darkest valley,
I will fear no evil,
   for you are with me;
your rod and your staff,
   they comfort me.

You prepare a table before me
   in the presence of my enemies.
You anoint my head with oil;
   my cup overflows.
Surely your goodness and love will follow me
   all the days of my life,
and I will dwell in the house of the Lord
forever.

Consider This

What happened to "the valley of the shadow of death"?

The NIV went too far with verse 4. "The darkest valley" just doesn't seem to do it justice, right?

Let's dig a little deeper. The Hebrew more accurately renders into English as a deep, dark, death-like shadow. So "darkest valley" may be just a bit understated perhaps. Why do I make so much of this? Because the most common rendering of "the valley of the shadow of death" is what makes this psalm so famous as a funeral text. This verse comforts the bereaved, so much so, that most people have little dealing with the psalm anywhere beyond reciting it at funerals.

Psalm 23 is a life text. In fact, it is an eternal life text—not as in after death—but as in a right here Jesus, right now Jesus, eternal life text. So let's try this homegrown amplified version: *Even though I walk through the deepest, darkest, shadow of death-like valley, I will fear no evil, for you are with me; your rod and your staff, they comfort me.*

You get my point. This could be the death of a loved one or it could be about a thousand other deepest, darkest, shadow of death-like valley situations life throws our way.

It's interesting how this Hebrew word occurs eighteen times in the Bible, ten of which come from the book of Job. Sounds about right. It also shows up in the famous prophecy of Isaiah: "The people walking in darkness have seen a great light; on those living in the land of deep darkness a light has dawned" (Isa. 9:2).

And all of this could be an adventure in missing the point if we don't get to the real point here. No matter how deep, dark, shadowy, and intolerably death-like the valley may be—no matter how slavish the addiction, how obsessive and compulsive the disorder, how terminal the cancer, how grievous the divorce, how painful the betrayal, how devastating the death—even of your only child—here's the point:

I will fear no evil.

It doesn't say I will not feel sadness or grieve horrifically or suffer depression or be angry at God or struggle to believe or even fear the worst possible outcome. It says:

I will fear no evil.

It doesn't say my worst nightmare will not happen or my marriage will survive or my kids will not have significant problems or the cancer will be cured or I will not fail the test or I won't have to go to rehab . . . again. It says:

I will fear no evil.

Now, that is a curiosity to me. *I will fear no evil.* Why that? It means Satan, demonic powers, and all the forces of evil and darkness cannot and will not prevail against you. It is one thing to lose the battle with cancer, another thing entirely to lose the war with Satan. Remember the Good Shepherd context of John 10:10—the most favorite Bible verse: "The thief comes only to steal and kill and destroy; I have come that they may have life, and have it to the full."

What if the threat is not evil? What if the real threat is the fear of evil? There is something deep within everyone of us—something primal and even ancient—that fears evil. What if it is this fear that brings us into anxiety and leads us into sin, which shields us from awareness of the presence of God, our Good Shepherd? What if it is our fear of evil that keeps us from the abundant life of Jesus—even in the midst of the deepest, darkest, shadowiest, deadliest valleys of life?

This is ponderous. I'll admit it. But I believe the Lord put it on my heart to say it—and this:

There is only one reason we can say, "I will fear no evil." It is not because evil is not powerful and all around us all the time. It is this: *for you are with me.*

And maybe that's what the rod and the staff are all about.
your rod and your staff,
they comfort me.
Maybe, at times, especially in these valleys, we need the fear of evil poked and prodded out of us. Maybe we need to be hooked by the staff and pulled back onto the path because of where our fear of evil is taking us.
Even though I walk
through the darkest valley,
I will fear no evil,
for you are with me;
your rod and your staff,
they comfort me.
People who say such things are learning not to be bullied by evil into fear. They know the two things more powerful than fear: faith and love. They know: "There is no fear in love. But perfect love drives out fear" (1 John 4:18a).
This is who the Shepherd is. This is what the Shepherd does. This is why we must know the Shepherd today more than we knew him yesterday—and why we will need to know him more tomorrow than we knew him today.

The Prayer

Father, I want to be a person who says such things. I confess, even beyond my awareness, something deep in me primally fears evil and it drives me in an incomprehensible way into the law of sin and death. But you, who are in me, are greater than he who is in the world (see 1 John 4:4). You, Jesus, are my Shepherd, my Good Shepherd. You are with me. I will fear no evil. And I welcome your rod and your staff. Come, Holy Spirit, and train me to be such a person of faith. I pray in Jesus' name, amen.

The Questions

- So how do you understand this ponderous thought today about the fear of evil? And how do you understand the comfort of the rod and the staff of the Good Shepherd?

27 . . . Know This Is How We Fight Our Battles

PSALM 23 | The Lord is my shepherd, I lack nothing.
    He makes me lie down in green pastures,
  he leads me beside quiet waters,
    he refreshes my soul.
  He guides me along the right paths
    for his name's sake.
  Even though I walk
    through the darkest valley,
  I will fear no evil,
    for you are with me;
  your rod and your staff,
    they comfort me.

You prepare a table before me
   in the presence of my enemies.
You anoint my head with oil;
   my cup overflows.
Surely your goodness and love will follow me
   all the days of my life,
and I will dwell in the house of the LORD
forever.

Consider This

You prepare a table before me
   in the presence of my enemies.

In the presence of enemies we might expect a battle. Instead, Jesus, our Good Shepherd, prepares a table for us. He sets a feast for us in the midst of our enemies in the middle of the battleground. And he is himself the feast.

One of my favorite recent songs of worship comes out of a community called UpperRoom in Dallas. It is called "Fight My Battles." Though it is one of the most repetitive songs I've ever sung, it's one I don't tire of repeating. It makes the biblical and theological connection between the table of the Lord and this table prepared for us in the presence of our enemies. Over and over and over we sing, "This is how I fight my battles," almost twenty times each time through the song, referencing the body and blood of Jesus and the weapons of praise and thanksgiving. After singing the song through five times and then another five for good measure, as worship leaders like to do, it comes to about one hundred repetitions of this one line: "This is how I fight my battles."

But is this how I actually fight my battles; sitting at the table of the Lord in the presence of my enemies in the deep dark valleys of life? This seems so passive. How can one be so relaxed and at peace in the presence of such threats? It raises the other refrain in the song, which repeats itself sixteen times: "It may look like I'm surrounded, but I'm surrounded by you."

But it doesn't stop there.

You anoint my head with oil;

It's interesting to think about the author of this psalm, David. When the prophet Samuel came to his house to anoint the next king of Israel, David was not even considered by his father as a candidate. He was out shepherding the sheep. Samuel sent for him and he turned out to be the Lord's choice as the next king: "So Samuel took the horn of oil and anointed him in the presence of his brothers, and from that day on the Spirit of the LORD came powerfully upon David" (1 Sam. 16:13).

Something tells me David remembered this anointing as he wrote the psalm.

It doesn't stop there. The extraordinary, extravagant blessing of the presence of God keeps leveling up.

my cup overflows.

More than enough. My memory goes to the famed wedding at Cana of Galilee when they ran out of wine. Jesus transformed water into wine to the tune of one hundred eighty gallons. Talk about cups overflowing! This is our God—above and beyond more than enough.

Remember where we began.

The Lord is my shepherd: I lack nothing.

He makes me lie down in green pastures: I lack nothing.

he leads me beside quiet waters: I lack nothing.

he refreshes my soul: I lack nothing.

He guides me along the right paths

for his name's sake: I lack nothing.

Even though I walk

through the darkest valley,

I will fear no evil,

for you are with me: I lack nothing.

your rod and your staff,

they comfort me: I lack nothing.

You prepare a table before me

in the presence of my enemies: I lack nothing.

You anoint my head with oil: I lack nothing.

my cup overflows: I lack nothing.

People who say such things know this is how we fight our battles. They know it may look like we're surrounded, but we're surrounded by God.

The Prayer

Father, I want to be a person who says such things. This is how I fight my battles. Let me say it and sing it until I get it and believe it. In your presence and by your provision, I lack nothing. Oh, how I want this declaration of faith to destroy my fear and define my life. Thank you for preparing such an extravagant table for me in the most difficult seasons of life. Thank you for anointing my head with the oil of your Spirit. Thank you for overflowing my cup. Come, Holy Spirit, and train me to be such a person of faith. I pray in Jesus' name, amen.

The Questions

- How is this journey through Psalm 23 calling out to you? Challenging you? Changing you?

28 . . . Recognize the Answers in Their Prayers

PSALM 23 | The Lᴏʀᴅ is my shepherd, I lack nothing.
  He makes me lie down in green pastures,
he leads me beside quiet waters,
  he refreshes my soul.
He guides me along the right paths
  for his name's sake.
Even though I walk
  through the darkest valley,
I will fear no evil,
  for you are with me;
your rod and your staff,
  they comfort me.

You prepare a table before me
  in the presence of my enemies.

You anoint my head with oil;
>   my cup overflows.
Surely your goodness and love will follow me
>   all the days of my life,
and I will dwell in the house of the LORD
forever.

Consider This

It's time to break camp and get back on the road, but what a treat this text has offered us; six days over six verses. We could spend another six weeks and still not exhaust the insights in the Twenty-Third Psalm.

This is part of the mysterious nature of Scripture. Each text has a fixed meaning and yet it keeps revealing more and more meaning; never new, but always fresh. The Word of God constantly speaks on different levels into our hearts and minds concerning the myriad multiple layers and multiple circumstances of our lives. It's why we are never done with a particular chapter or verse of Scripture. Though the text of Scripture is as fixed as the sun and though it means today the same thing it meant when it was first inspired and written, there is always more of ourselves to give and more of God to receive.

We began with our Good Shepherd in front of us, leading the way. Today we close with this:

Surely your goodness and love will follow me
all the days of my life,

This is the nature of the glorious greatness of the goodness of God: ever before us, ever behind us, and ever with us. It reminds us of another great psalm—Psalm 139—and these words: "You hem me in behind and before, and you lay your hand upon me" (v. 5). It reminds us of the great prayer at the heart of St. Patrick's Breastplate:

Christ, be with me, Christ before me, Christ behind me,
Christ in me, Christ beneath me, Christ above me,
Christ on my right, Christ on my left, Christ where I lie,
    Christ where I sit,
Christ where I arise, Christ in the heart of every man
    who thinks of me,
Christ in the mouth of every man who speaks of me,
Christ in every eye that sees me, Christ in every ear that
    hears me.

And as if all of these blessings for "all the days of my life" were not enough, there's yet more:

and I will dwell in the house of the LORD forever.

With my oldest son in college and my two daughters at driving age, I still get to drive my youngest son, Sam, to school every day. I have always tried to lay claim to the time in the car for versing the Word of God together. It's a part of that Deuteronomy 6 effort to "talk about them when you sit at home and when you walk along the road, when you lie down and when you get up" (v. 7). For years now, on most days, we recite the Twenty-Third Psalm back and forth together. All at once simple and sublime, Psalm 23 is our clarity, our certainty, and our comfort. This is the prayer, for which to pray it, is to know it answered.

The version we have "rememberized" is below. (Sam's part is in italics.)

The Lord is my Shepherd: *I lack nothing.* He makes me lie down in green pastures. *He leads me beside still waters.* He restores my soul. *He leads me in paths of righteousness*, for his name's sake. *Yea though I walk through the valley of the shadow of death*, I will fear no evil, *for you are with me.* Your rod and your staff, they comfort me. *You prepare a table before me* in the presence of my enemies. *You anoint my head with oil.* My cup overflows. *Surely goodness and mercy will follow me* all the days of my life, *and I will dwell in the house of the Lord*, forever.

People who say such things know there's no better prayer than the one which carries its own answer.

The Prayer

Father, I want to be a person who says such things. Thank you for Psalm 23. Thank you for a prayer that declares its own answer. Etch these words in the lining of my soul. Let them be for me like a perfectly fitting garment. Give me the confidence I need not to even look back, because I know goodness and mercy are following close on my heels. Come, Holy Spirit, and train me to be such a person of faith. I pray in Jesus' name, amen.

The Questions

- Could God really be this good? Do you ever marvel at a sheer truth that seems too good to be true? It's true, you know. It really is.

29 . . . Receive by Revelation

GALATIANS 1:11–12 | I want you to know, brothers and sisters, that the gospel I preached is not of human origin. I did not receive it from any man, nor was I taught it; rather, I received it by revelation from Jesus Christ.

Consider This

Has the gospel of Jesus Christ been revealed to you? I am not asking if you have heard it or received teaching about it. I am asking if it has been revealed to you.

This reminds me of the famous encounter between Jesus and Peter; the one we know as Peter's confession:

> "But what about you?" he asked. "Who do you say I am?"
> Simon Peter answered, "You are the Messiah, the Son of the living God."
> Jesus replied, "Blessed are you, Simon son of Jonah, for this was not revealed to you by flesh and blood, but by my Father in heaven." (Matt. 16:15–17)

For something to be revealed to us means more than just basic comprehension of the information or intellectually understanding it (though it may or may not include this). It means we have perceived the truth and reality of something in a deeper way.

It reminds us of Jesus' encounter with the elite religious leader, Nicodemus, who was not only impressed with his teaching but with his miraculous signs. Clearly, Jesus indicated this was not what he was looking for:

> Jesus answered, "Very truly I tell you, no one can enter the kingdom of God unless they are born of water and the Spirit. Flesh gives birth to flesh, but the Spirit gives birth to spirit." (John 3:5–6)

We are dealing with the realm of awakening here. It is not in our control:

> "You should not be surprised at my saying, 'You must be born again.' The wind blows wherever it pleases. You hear its sound, but you cannot tell where it comes from or where it is going. So it is with everyone born of the Spirit." (John 3:7–8)

Did we think the gospel could be reduced to a set of teachings, doctrinal propositions, or precepts to which one could assent, repeat a prayer, and be considered to have accepted Jesus? Perhaps it might be a useful way to invite people to *start* following Jesus, though it doesn't seem like he did it that way. The long and short of what I am saying is that we can't reveal Jesus to other people; only God can do that. We must invite people to follow Jesus and pray for them to be awakened, but only the Spirit can do the revealing. It is not just a one-time thing, but an ongoing reality. That's what Paul seemed to be about:

> I keep asking that the God of our Lord Jesus Christ, the glorious Father, may give you the Spirit of wisdom and revelation, so that you may know him better. (Eph. 1:17)

In our ongoing work with Seedbed and New Room, we have done a lot of praying, conferencing, discerning, listening, and thinking concerning this whole concept of awakening. We've been quietly hammering out a definition of sorts. We are up to 188 words and eight sentences so far, but none of them are more powerful than the first one, which I will share here:

> Awakening is the outcome of encountering Jesus, by which the love of God the Father is poured into our hearts by the Holy Spirit . . .

This is not only the main thing of the Christian faith; it is the ongoing thing. In fact, dare I say, it is the only thing.

I want you to know, brothers and sisters, that the gospel I preached is not of human origin. I did not receive it from any man, nor was I taught it; rather, I received it by revelation from Jesus Christ.

People who say such things know awakening comes not by information or cogitation or even explanation—helpful as these things can be to the process. Awakening comes by revelation through encountering Jesus.

The Prayer

Father, I want to be a person who says such things. Thank you for revealing your Son, Jesus Christ, to me. Thank you for waking me up to your gospel. I want to know Jesus better, so I pray you continue to open the eyes of my heart and sustain the awakening in me until I, myself, become an agent of your awakening in the lives of others. Come, Holy Spirit, and train me to be such a person of faith. I pray in Jesus' name, amen.

The Questions

- What is your awakening story? How is it continuing to unfold? Where is the awakening happening in your life at the moment?

. . . Fear God More than People

30

EXODUS 1:15–21 | The king of Egypt said to the Hebrew midwives, whose names were Shiphrah and Puah, "When you are helping the Hebrew women during childbirth on the delivery stool, if you see that the baby is a boy, kill him; but if it is a girl, let her live." The midwives, however, feared God and did not do what the king of Egypt had told them to do; they let the boys live. Then the king of Egypt summoned the midwives and asked them, "Why have you done this? Why have you let the boys live?"

The midwives answered Pharaoh, "Hebrew women are not like Egyptian women; they are vigorous and give birth before the midwives arrive."

So God was kind to the midwives and the people increased and became even more numerous. And because the midwives feared God, he gave them families of their own.

Consider This

Coming back around to our story line, we find ourselves in the epic story of Exodus. Eight verses in we get this fateful word: "Then a new king, to whom Joseph meant nothing, came to power in Egypt" (Ex. 1:8).

Everything changed. Enter cruel slavery. Enter genocide. The Israelites went from great favor to grave fear in the span of days. Life can be like that. It's why we do not trust in the temporality of prosperity. Everything can change, literally overnight. We trust God. Pandemics come and go. Stock markets rise and fall. Fortunes are won and lost. Nations flourish and collapse. The God of Israel, who is the Father of our Lord Jesus Christ, never fails.

The king of Egypt said to the Hebrew midwives, whose names were Shiphrah and Puah . . .

Fascinating! The king of Egypt is speaking to the Israelite midwives. He's ordering the midwives to murder the boy babies immediately upon their birth. Then we get this bit:

The midwives, however, feared God and did not do what the king of Egypt had told them to do; they let the boys live.

The midwives knew the king's word was law, but they knew even more that God's Word is truth. And they knew they dare not disobey God in the interest of appeasing Pharaoh. They feared God more than they feared man. Sometimes obedience to the Word of God must mean defiance of the laws of Pharaoh.

The midwives answered Pharaoh, "Hebrew women are not like Egyptian women; they are vigorous and give birth before the midwives arrive."

History is replete with examples of fearful rulers, unjust laws, and oppressive rulings resulting in disastrous outcomes for human beings. (*Dred Scott v. Sandford, Korematsu v. United States, Roe v. Wade,* and *Obergefell v. Hodges* come to mind.) We now live in an age of the great confusion; a day when things long settled are undone; when eternal verities are discarded with the stroke of a pen. It will undoubtedly be followed by an age of great darkness and brokenness. Those who sow into the wind reap the whirlwind. The good news, though, is the great darkness will be followed by a great awakening, the likes of which has not been seen in centuries.

The secret to a great nation is not so much in its leaders, be they presidents, legislators, or judges. The secret is in the God-fearing, faith-filled citizens of the kingdom who are not afraid to defy the dictates of the cultural elite and the avant-garde trends of the spirit of the age; especially as it comes to the enormous cost it will mean for human beings when the Word of God is defied. They do so by humbly sowing, even tearfully, in the midst of confusion, on the eve of darkness and all in the sure confidence of the coming awakening.

Thank God for Shiphrah and Puah, those courageous Israelite midwives. They get far more than honorable mention in the history books. They turn out to be the history makers. They always do. May their tribe increase.

The Prayer

Father, I want to be a person who says such things. I want to be humble and yet courageous. I renounce the spirit of the age and I stand on the Word of God. Transform my anger at all the confusion around us into a holy lament. And transform my malcontent with the problems around me into a holy discontent with the problems within me. My hope is not in political leaders, though I pray for them. My hope is in Jesus Christ and his coming kingdom. Today, I sow for a great awakening. Come, Holy Spirit, and train me to be such a person of faith. I pray in Jesus' name, amen.

The Question

- How might we resist the spirit of the age, not with our anger and outrage, but in the power of the Holy Spirit with humility and courage?

31 . . . Do Not Choose the Lesser of Two Evils

EXODUS 2:1–4 | Now a man of the tribe of Levi married a Levite woman, and she became pregnant and gave birth to a son. When she saw that he was a fine child, she hid him for three months. But when she could hide him no longer, she got a papyrus basket for him and coated it with tar and pitch. Then she placed the child in it and put it among the reeds along the bank of the Nile. His sister stood at a distance to see what would happen to him.

Consider This

Get a picture in your mind of hundreds of young men carrying their infant sons in their arms, walking out to the river bank of the Nile, and throwing their sons into the river to drown. I'm sorry to even ask you to see such a sight. It happened. This is the world we live in.

I mean, what were they supposed to do? Yesterday, I failed to point out how Pharaoh instituted another infanticidal law: "Then Pharaoh gave this order to all his people: 'Every Hebrew boy that is born you must throw into the Nile, but let every girl live'" (Ex. 1:22).

It is a choice of evils. Do the parents suffer the death of their child or should they risk being caught (at which point, they would lose not only the child, but perhaps the mother and father too as a punishment; or maybe even the rest of the children)? We are dealing with pure evil here.

One of the most successful and seductive strategies of evil is to convince us our only choice is evil—that we must choose between the lesser of two evils. I struggle to admit it, because I know just how real the choice of evil dilemmas can be, but to choose the lesser of two evils is still to choose evil. I am coming to believe the choice-of-evils defense (called so because it is a way of defending one's evil choices) is not so much a logical fallacy for Christians as it is a theological fallacy. Why? Because with God, there must always be another option. While it may not always seem like a good alternative, it must be a non-evil option. That's what we see in today's text.

When she saw that he was a fine child, she hid him for three months.

She saw the inestimable potential in the life of a child given by God. Something in her knew this child belonged to God. But doesn't every parent see a fine child when they look at a newborn? Something about the vision of this mother was different. It's a good word to us parents—we must ask God to grant us the vision to see our children as he sees them. She refused to kill her baby boy. She knew there must be another way.

But when she could hide him no longer, she got a papyrus basket for him and coated it with tar and pitch. Then she placed the child in it and put it among the reeds along the bank of the Nile.

This choice was mortifying, yet it was creative and full of love and care. Her choice created the possibility of something different happening; something new and unexpected. Sure, it was fraught with peril, but it was not a lesser-of-evils choice. It was a choice of greater faith—one that extended life as far as she possibly could—a choice creating the opportunity for all the unpredictable possibilities of God to work.

One of the dark strategies of the spirit of the age of the great confusion in which we live is to bully God-fearing citizens of the kingdom into an ever-evolving choice-of-evils dilemma. We must come to grips with the truth.

Beneath the choice-of-evils scenario is a choice of fears. Who will we fear more: evil or God? We agreed last week in Psalm 23 that the fear of evil is the path of destruction. When we fear evil we invariably resort to choosing the lesser of evils. When we fear God, we resist evil and we choose the way of greater faith—the way most often invisible to the naked eye. Note the plaque on the wall of the celebrated Hall of Faith: "By faith Moses' parents hid him for three months after he was born, because they saw he was no ordinary child, and they were not afraid of the king's edict" (Heb. 11:23).

Let's pause here on the bank of the Nile as the tiny Ark of Faith floats into the water's current, holding an infant slave condemned to death, carrying all the hopes of the future of the kingdom of God. We will take big sister's hand as we watch.

His sister stood at a distance to see what would happen to him.

The Prayer

Father, I want to be a person who says such things. Grant me courage, Lord, to not only resist evil but to rebuke the ever-so-reasonable invitation to choose evil under the auspices of it somehow ever being lesser. This seems impossible in this world, and yet nothing is impossible with you. I know the choice of greater faith will come at a cost to myself, my reputation, and my respectability. I declare in faith, I fear no evil. I fear God. And, even more, I love you, God. Come, Holy Spirit, and train me to be such a person of faith. I pray in Jesus' name, amen.

The Questions

- Where does your mind run in a practical way as it comes to being pressed into choosing the lesser of two evils? Can you see where you have succumbed to it in the past? What will it take to leave that whole paradigm behind and shift into the choice of the greater alternatives of faith?

32 . . . Choose Surrender over Resignation

EXODUS 2:5–10 | Then Pharaoh's daughter went down to the Nile to bathe, and her attendants were walking along the riverbank. She saw the basket among the reeds and sent her female slave to get it. She opened it and saw the baby. He was crying, and she felt sorry for him. "This is one of the Hebrew babies," she said.

Then his sister asked Pharaoh's daughter, "Shall I go and get one of the Hebrew women to nurse the baby for you?"

"Yes, go," she answered. So the girl went and got the baby's mother. Pharaoh's daughter said to her, "Take this baby and nurse him for me, and I will pay you." So the woman took the baby and nursed him. When the child grew older, she took him to Pharaoh's daughter and he became her son. She named him Moses, saying, "I drew him out of the water."

Consider This

Astonishing!

Remember this scripture from Joseph: "You intended to harm me, but God intended it for good to accomplish what is now being done, the saving of many lives" (Gen. 50:20).

In case you missed it: Pharaoh's daughter came to the Nile to bathe and spotted the tiny Ark of Faith. She sent her slave over to investigate, and—just like that—this infant slave, condemned to death by her Pharaoh father, was in her arms.

It gets better. Remember big sister? We were holding her hand as she watched the baby float into the reeds. Well, sister sidled up to Pharaoh's daughter with a quite strategic solution:

"Shall I go and get one of the Hebrew women to nurse the baby for you?"

"Yes, go," she answered. So the girl went and got the baby's mother.

The plot keeps turning, and eases into the category of "Truth is stranger than fiction." You can't make this up.

Pharaoh's daughter said to her, "Take this baby and nurse him for me, and I will pay you." So the woman took the baby and nursed him.

Pharaoh's daughter had agreed to pay the baby's mother to nurse her own baby; the one she surrendered to God into the Nile in her tiny Ark of Faith just hours before. You know the word for this: *astonishing!*

When the child grew older, she took him to Pharaoh's daughter and he became her son. She named him Moses, saying, "I drew him out of the water."

So many things could be said about this. I will seize the moment to make this point: A choice of evils always leads to a spirit of weak resignation. The choice of greater faith always inspires a heart of strong surrender.

In an age of great confusion—with an almost constant choice of lesser evils—the tendency to succumb to weak resignation will abound. Everyone around will be doing it; giving in, giving up, and giving over the dominion of truth to the spirit of the age. The seduction, of course, will be anger, outrage, and fighting back. That is a trap as well. The way forward is not to battle with evil, enemies, or even well-intentioned opponents who become the unwitting advocates of darkness. The way forward is to deal with God alone in the spirit of deep, strong, uncompromising surrender to him.

Moses' parents did not succumb to the choice of evils, nor did they attempt to do battle with Pharaoh—whom they did not fear. Instead, they made a deeper surrender to God.

What Pharaoh intended for evil, God turned into good. Through these two exceedingly obscure and unimportant people at this very obscure moment in the history of the world, we get one of the most famous people who ever lived: Moses, the one drawn up out of the water.

Remember that the next time you think your choice or your voice or your courageous action doesn't matter.

Remember that in the present struggle in your own life, the one that has you tired beyond tired and ready to quit. Don't give up or give in to weak resignation. Surrender to Jesus. He's right here, right now.

The Prayer

Father, I want to be a person who says such things. Thank you for this astonishing true story. You inspire courage and obedience in me. Teach me the way of the choice of greater faith in the little things and in the seemingly small ways when no one is looking. Orient my mind and heart directly to you and not to the need to impress or appease others. I confess my own tendency toward weak resignation. Train my heart to walk in this way of deep surrender to you alone. Come, Holy Spirit, and train me to be such a person of faith. I pray in Jesus' name, amen.

The Questions

- Are you astonished by this story today? How are you inspired to renounce the spirit of weak resignation to your circumstances and to surrender to God in bold faith?

. . . Do the Will of God in the Ways of God

33

EXODUS 2:11–15 | One day, after Moses had grown up, he went out to where his own people were and watched them at their hard labor. He saw an Egyptian beating a Hebrew, one of his own people. Looking this way and that and seeing no one, he killed the Egyptian and hid him in the sand. The next day he went out and saw two Hebrews fighting. He asked the one in the wrong, "Why are you hitting your fellow Hebrew?"

The man said, "Who made you ruler and judge over us? Are you thinking of killing me as you killed the Egyptian?" Then Moses was afraid and thought, "What I did must have become known."

When Pharaoh heard of this, he tried to kill Moses, but Moses fled from Pharaoh and went to live in Midian, where he sat down by a well.

Consider This

There is the will of God and then there are the ways of God. When the will of God is not executed in the ways of God, it leads to something other than the will of God. Today's text is a case in point.

The will of God would oppose the cruel and unjust treatment of slaves, right? Backing up a step, the will of God would oppose slavery altogether, right? Moses intervened against an Egyptian slave master who was abusing an Israelite slave. So far so good, right? He took it a step further and killed the Egyptian. That's where the road forked on the will of God. There is a way of dealing with cruelty, injustice, and even abuse. When one does evil to defeat evil it still leaves us with evil. The right thing done in the wrong way is the wrong thing, right?

What happens when a person does the right thing in the wrong way? They lose credibility. It diminishes their authority. It destroys their witness. Isn't that what happened with Moses here?

The next day he went out and saw two Hebrews fighting. He asked the one in the wrong, "Why are you hitting your fellow Hebrew?" The man said, "Who made you ruler and judge over us? Are you thinking of killing me as you killed the Egyptian?"

The end does not justify the means. It proved costly for Moses, sending him from his palace of extreme privilege into what would be a very long exile. It would be in these years that Moses would become familiar with the ways of God; profoundly prepared to pursue the will of God in the deliverance of the people of God.

When Pharaoh heard of this, he tried to kill Moses, but Moses fled from Pharaoh and went to live in Midian, where he sat down by a well.

The good news is the will of God will not be thwarted. Even despite our broken ways, God works all things together for good (see Romans 8:28). He will not be surprised, outflanked, or thwarted—ever. It may take longer, centuries even, but he has time on his side.

The Prayer

Father, I want to be a person who says such things. I want to know your will, but even more so, I want to learn your ways. Because your ways are not my ways, I hereby renounce my ways and submit myself to learning yours. Thank you for the way you so clearly demonstrate your ways through your Son, Jesus. I will follow him. Come, Holy Spirit, and train me to be such a person of faith. I pray in Jesus' name, amen.

The Questions

- Have you ever done what you understood to be the will of God yet not in the ways of God? What happened? How did that go?

34 ... Trust God with Difficult Circumstances

EXODUS 2:16–25 | Now a priest of Midian had seven daughters, and they came to draw water and fill the troughs to water their father's flock. Some shepherds came along and drove them away, but Moses got up and came to their rescue and watered their flock.

When the girls returned to Reuel their father, he asked them, "Why have you returned so early today?"

They answered, "An Egyptian rescued us from the shepherds. He even drew water for us and watered the flock."

"And where is he?" Reuel asked his daughters. "Why did you leave him? Invite him to have something to eat."

Moses agreed to stay with the man, who gave his daughter Zipporah to Moses in marriage. Zipporah gave birth to a son, and Moses named him Gershom, saying, "I have become a foreigner in a foreign land."

During that long period, the king of Egypt died. The Israelites groaned in their slavery and cried out, and their cry for help because of their slavery went up to God. God heard their groaning and he remembered his covenant with Abraham, with Isaac and with Jacob. So God looked on the Israelites and was concerned about them.

Consider This

Life is what happens when you are making other plans.

Moses' life seemed to have taken a detour. The text describes this season of Moses' life as a "long period."

He thought he did the right thing back in Egypt in coming to the defense of an Israelite slave. No sooner than he left Egypt, he found himself in another confrontation with a group of rogue shepherds trying to attack a band of seven defenseless sisters. Moses is a good egg, but he is lost, and life goes on. Though good things happen to him, including finding a wife and having a son, he still finds himself in exile. The name he gave his son tells the story.

Zipporah gave birth to a son, and Moses named him Gershom, saying, "I have become a foreigner in a foreign land."

He must have wondered to himself, *Why this? Am I being punished? What did I do wrong?* He had been exiled twice; first from his own people, the Israelites, and then from his adopted people, the Egyptians. He had gone from the privilege of the palace to herding sheep in Midian. The name Gershom says it all:

"I have become a foreigner in a foreign land."

Have you ever felt exiled from your life; stuck in a moment you can't get out of? Things are not turning out like you planned. Something or someone intervenes in your best-laid plans and a promising path turns toward what seems to be an endless exile. "Where did I go wrong?" you ask. You find yourself saying things like, *"I have become a foreigner in a foreign land."*

Here's the good news. When you are doing your best to follow Jesus and it feels like you are exiled from your life, you are not being punished. You are being prepared.

At the same time Moses is wondering aloud about what happened to his best life, another conversational drama is playing out one hundred miles away—as in, "Meanwhile, back at the ranch . . ."

During that long period, the king of Egypt died. The Israelites groaned in their slavery and cried out, and their cry for help because of their slavery went up to God. God heard their groaning and he remembered his covenant with Abraham, with Isaac and with Jacob. So God looked on the Israelites and was concerned about them.

It can feel like life is an endless losing game of checkers, until we discover it was not a game of checkers at all. God was playing chess. And he never loses.

In times like these, we must exchange the "Why me?" question for the "Why this?" inquiry. We must turn out the lights on our pity party and open our hearts to the curriculum of circumstances through which God is preparing us for a future season we cannot yet see, much less imagine.

"I have become a foreigner in a foreign land."

It may be a lot closer to home than we realize.

The Prayer

Father, I want to be a person who says such things. Thank you for all the ways you take hardships and difficult circumstances and weave them into your plan for my good. Because of this, I can thank you for even the hardest of times. I offer up my circumstances, turning away from my victimhood, my bitterness, and even letting go of my own dreams and best-laid plans. I trust you, and because I trust you I trust your path. You are the God who can turn lost into found and exile into home. Prepare me, Lord. Prepare me. Come, Holy Spirit, and train me to be such a person of faith. I pray in Jesus' name, amen.

The Questions

- How about it? Ever felt exiled from your life? Maybe even now? How might you make the turn toward trusting God to do something new in the midst of it? What might that look like?

. . . Know the Difference between Their Importance and Their Worth

35

EXODUS 3:1 | Now Moses was tending the flock of Jethro his father-in-law, the priest of Midian, and he led the flock to the far side of the wilderness and came to Horeb, the mountain of God.

Consider This

The mountain of God is at the far side of the wilderness.

Did you catch that? The mountain of God is at the far side of the wilderness. It rings true, doesn't it? This is physical geography, yet it is also spiritual geography.

From a condemned infant slave to the palace of Pharaoh, Moses enjoyed extreme privilege in the first season of his life. From the peak of power to the wilderness of Midian, he experienced great obscurity in the second season of his life. The text is careful to tell he herded not his own sheep but those of his father-in-law, Jethro (referred to as Reuel in previous verses). These incredible shifts of fortune pale in comparison to what happened next.

After decades of punching the clock, Moses found himself in the midst of another long day, perhaps daydreaming about retirement, if there was such a thing in those days. He was probably somewhere between seventy and eighty, somewhere between death and dying, somewhere between cynicism and nothing to look forward to.

Now Moses was tending the flock of Jethro his father-in-law, the priest of Midian, and he led the flock to the far side of the wilderness and came to Horeb, the mountain of God.

It's the far side of the wilderness. And it is the mountain of God. He had lived some forty years in this valley of vision, preparing for this next moment, which would open the door into a pilgrimage to another mountain of God, Mount Sinai, and yet another forty years of wilderness wandering.

It is easy to look back from the vantage point of the whole story and marvel at the greatness of Moses and his single importance to the will of God; yet the only reason we even know about his life is because of a late-life encounter with God at a bush on fire yet not burning up. Biographies aren't typically written until the end of one's story. I wonder how many other shepherds passed by the same burning bush and didn't even notice. We could just as well be reading about them instead.

There was something about Moses. He was different. We remember his extraordinary life, yet we tend to brush over the extraordinary difficulties of his life. By my math, he wandered in the wilderness for a solid eighty of his one hundred twenty years.

Sometimes it takes a long season in the wilderness to learn the difference between one's importance and their worth. Sometimes it takes being sidelined by failure or exiled by circumstances or the meaninglessness of a menial job to remind us that our worth doesn't come from what we can do for God but from who we are in Christ.

I'm writing to a college student who needs to know Jesus doesn't need their skills and résumé to change the world. He wants your heart.

I'm writing to a young-ish mother who feels as though she has lost herself in diapers and dishes. Jesus is not interested in the former dreams of your earlier life. He wants your heart right now.

I'm writing to a middle-aged pastor who is angry at the mediocrity of the church and determined to do something about it. Jesus is not interested in your tireless ambition to make him great. He wants your heart.

I'm writing to a retired person who has mistaken their dreams for a relatively comfortable life. Jesus is not interested in fortunes and facelifts. He wants your heart.

I'm writing to myself with all my self-important notions of grandeur to sow for a great awakening. Jesus is not interested in my noble ambitions. He wants my heart.

If these words feel crushing, as they do for me, it's probably because they need to. This is the far side of the wilderness after all, the place they call the mountain of God. It's the altar where our earthbound dreams come to die that the vision of heaven might be birthed in our hearts—anew, afresh, or maybe for the very first time.

The Prayer

Father, I want to be a person who says such things. I want you to have my heart. I am weary of my own best ideas and plans. I'm tired of walking in circles. I am only willing to wander if it is your will, for then it will be my calling and privilege. Lead me to the far side of the wilderness; indeed, to the mountain of God. Come, Holy Spirit, and train me to be such a person of faith. I pray in Jesus' name, amen.

The Question

- How have you come to a deepened understanding of the different between your importance and your worth?

. . . Are on Fire, but Not Burned Up

36

EXODUS 3:2–3 | There the angel of the Lord appeared to him in flames of fire from within a bush. Moses saw that though the bush was on fire it did not burn up. So Moses thought, "I will go over and see this strange sight—why the bush does not burn up."

Consider This

Ten words have rocked my world for the better part of the last ten years: *the bush was on fire it did not burn up.*

This is one of the famous stories of Scripture—the Burning Bush. The more famous the story, the more we think we've got it and the less we return for closer examination. The mystery is not in the burning part. It is in the not burning up part.

The burning caught Moses' eye. The not burning up captured his attention.

So Moses thought, "I will go over and see this strange sight— why the bush does not burn up."

Burning bushes are a phenomenon of nature, but burning bushes not burning up—clearly supernatural. Ordinary bush. Extraordinary fire.

I see this text as a profound sign of the calling of every Christian—to be on fire but not consumed.

> John answered them all, "I baptize you with water. But one who is more powerful than I will come, the straps

of whose sandals I am not worthy to untie. He will baptize you with the Holy Spirit and fire." (Luke 3:16)

The Word became flesh and made his dwelling among us. We have seen his glory, the glory of the one and only Son, who came from the Father, full of grace and truth. (John 1:14)

Very truly I tell you, whoever believes in me will do the works I have been doing, and they will do even greater things than these, because I am going to the Father. (John 14:12)

"But you will receive power when the Holy Spirit comes on you; and you will be my witnesses in Jerusalem, and in all Judea and Samaria, and to the ends of the earth." (Acts 1:8)

When the day of Pentecost came, they were all together in one place. Suddenly a sound like the blowing of a violent wind came from heaven and filled the whole house where they were sitting. They saw what seemed to be tongues of fire that separated and came to rest on each of them. (Acts 2:1–3)

I have been crucified with Christ and I no longer live, but Christ lives in me. The life I now live in the body, I live by faith in the Son of God, who loved me and gave himself for me. (Gal. 2:20)

For God, who said, "Let light shine out of darkness," made his light shine in our hearts to give us the light of the knowledge of God's glory displayed in the face of Christ.

But we have this treasure in jars of clay to show that this all-surpassing power is from God and not from us. (2 Cor. 4:6–7)

I see in this burning bush the great mystery of holiness: ordinary human beings filled with the supernatural fire of the Holy Spirit.

The woman was on fire but she did not burn up. The man was on fire but he did not burn up.

This burning-bush reality in your life will run as deep as your desire for it.

Whenever that happens, this happens:

So Moses thought, "I will go over and see this strange sight— why the bush does not burn up."

Imagine a church filled with these kinds of people. People who say such things . . .

The Prayer

Father, I want to be a person who says such things. I want the holy fire of the holy love of God to fill my life in such a way that it becomes a humble spectacle of glory; a bush on fire yet not burning up. I know it will mean first being refined by this fire. Let it be with me according to your Word. Come,

Holy Spirit, and train me to be such a person of faith. I pray in Jesus' name, amen.

The Question

- How deep is your desire for this burning-bush reality in your life?

 # 37 ... Shrug off Their Slumbering Spirit

EXODUS 3:4–6 | When the LORD saw that he had gone over to look, God called to him from within the bush, "Moses! Moses!"

And Moses said, "Here I am."

"Do not come any closer," God said. "Take off your sandals, for the place where you are standing is holy ground." Then he said, "I am the God of your father, the God of Abraham, the God of Isaac and the God of Jacob." At this, Moses hid his face, because he was afraid to look at God.

Consider This

On the far side of the wilderness we come to the mountain of God, and God does not disappoint.

Moses' attention, riveted by the strange phenomenon captured in the ten words we explored yesterday, "The bush was on fire it did not burn up," walked toward the bush to investigate.

*When the L*ORD *saw that he had gone over to look, God called to him from within the bush, "Moses! Moses!"*

What does one do when they hear their name called twice by an unburning bush? One responds in good biblical form: *And Moses said, "Here I am."*

I wonder how it might change the shape of my days if the first words from my mouth each morning were these, "Here I am." Though I may not audibly hear it, these words would be spoken in faith that God is indeed calling my name.

"Do not come any closer," God said. "Take off your sandals, for the place where you are standing is holy ground."

This whole affair with the unburning bush was exceptional and extraordinary, a one-time deal. After all, there is only one burning bush in the whole Bible, right? It's easy to marvel at these kinds of stories and then dismiss them as having little bearing on our own lives and experience.

It is true these stories with Abraham and Moses and so forth are unique in the history of the world. They are in many ways unrepeatable. The Bible does not intend to normalize the voice of God coming from a bush on fire but not burning up. God did extraordinary things at particular times with unique people back then, but not so much anymore, right? Wrong.

We live in the age of the Holy Spirit, who is being poured out all over the world, on all flesh, women and men, giving vision to the young and dreams to the old. There is a famous and oft-quoted verse of poetry from Elizabeth Barrett Browning that fits here:

> Earth's crammed with heaven,
> And every common bush afire with God,
> But only he who sees takes off his shoes;
> The rest sit round and pluck blackberries.

Our problem is sleepwalking. We have lost our expectancy of hearing from God in the early morning and seeing God in our days. The active prevenient working of the Holy Spirit in every person we encounter so easily slips out of our awareness. We forget that we are the burning bush—ordinary human beings illuminated with the fiery love of God. The Spirit of God is renewing the face of the earth, right here, right now. All ground is holy ground.

Only he who sees takes off his shoes.

Then he said, "I am the God of your father, the God of Abraham, the God of Isaac and the God of Jacob." At this, Moses hid his face, because he was afraid to look at God.

The Prayer

Father, I want to be a person who says such things. I confess how easily I slip into slumber. I wake up only to hit the proverbial snooze bar in my spirit. My vision gets so blinded by my circumstances. Wake me up. Give me ears to hear and eyes to see. In this moment, I speak aloud in faith, "Here am I." Come, Holy Spirit, and train me to be such a person of faith. I pray in Jesus' name, amen.

The Questions

- Do you think it could be possible that you are sleep-walking in this season of your life? Would you be open to the possibility that this could be true? Only those who are open dare ask God to wake them up.

. . . Never Retire

38

EXODUS 3:7–10 | The LORD said, "I have indeed seen the misery of my people in Egypt. I have heard them crying out because of their slave drivers, and I am concerned about their suffering. So I have come down to rescue them from the hand of the Egyptians and to bring them up out of that land into a good and spacious land, a land flowing with milk and honey—the home of the Canaanites, Hittites, Amorites, Perizzites, Hivites and Jebusites. And now the cry of the Israelites has reached me, and I have seen the way the Egyptians are oppressing them. So now, go. I am sending you to Pharaoh to bring my people the Israelites out of Egypt."

Consider This

I love what God doesn't say to Moses. He doesn't say, "Moses, I love you and have a wonderful plan for your life." He says, in fact, "I want your life for my plan."

Notice the verbiage in today's text: *"I have seen . . . I have heard . . . I am concerned . . . I have come down . . ."*

Moses was likely excited to hear the details of how God was going to solve this vexing problem of the enslavement of the Israelites. *Finally,* he must have been thinking to himself, *God is finally going to intervene in this abominable mess and save our people.* After all this demonstrative reporting, we get this sudden, dramatic shift:

So now, go. I am sending you . . .

Moses must have thought, *You must have the wrong Moses, here.* He must have thought, *That ship has sailed in my life.* At this point in his life he was out to pasture, in every sense of the term. Why would God come to an assisted living community to find a candidate to deliver a nation from the oppressive rule of a cruel dictator?

The better question may be this one: Why wouldn't God do this? Isn't it just like God to do just this kind of thing?

There are still places in the world where to be old is to be revered and set apart as the elders. The idea of putting them out to pasture would be anathema. The aging are the most experienced, the wisest, most spiritually mature members of any community. At the same time, they have the most discretionary time and, in many cases, the most wealth. Still, in this culture, they are increasingly sidelined, rotated off of boards, and encouraged to vacate positions of leadership so younger people can have a turn. At the same time, they are asked to step aside and write checks. It's wrong. I am beginning to think of these years between sixty and heaven as one's kingdom prime— comprising what could be the most fruitful season of one's life.

Youth and young adulthood are filled with idealism. The tests of midlife leads to an overabundance of realism. But what of old age? That is the question. The mature state of realism is just another name for cynicism. There is a higher way; the antithesis of cynicism really: dreams. On the day of Pentecost, Peter proclaimed the prophecy of Joel fulfilled, which declared that the aged will dream dreams (see Acts 2:17; Joel 2:28).

"So now, go. I am sending you to Pharaoh to bring my people the Israelites out of Egypt."

Old age (whatever old means) is not a season to retire. Okay, sure, quit your job if you want and can. You just can't retire. Your kingdom prime is ahead of you. This is a season to become wildly open to the dreams of God. It starts with the preferred biblical response to God: "Here I am!"

The Prayer

Father, I want to be a person who says such things. Thank you for your close attention to the affairs of this world. You see and hear and are concerned and you have come down so profoundly in your Son and your Spirit. You are forever with us, right here and right now. Thank you for believing in people enough to call out to us and bring us into your plan. I want to be more and more open to your plan. I want my life to be about your plan, whatever it is, come what may. Come, Holy Spirit, and train me to be such a person of faith. I pray in Jesus' name, amen.

The Questions

- Are you in the category of people I speak to today? How does what I am saying impact you? If you are not in the aging category, does this positively (and at least biblically) impact how you see the aging and their potential in the kingdom?

39 ... Transition from No, to Maybe, to Yes

EXODUS 3:11 | But Moses said to God, "Who am I that I should go to Pharaoh and bring the Israelites out of Egypt?"

Consider This

Just one verse today? I know. I know. It's like I've come to a complete stop right here at the unburning bush, haven't I? But . . . isn't that the point?

The Bible wants what happened on its pages to keep on happening as its pages are turned. The aspiration of the inspired text is to combust into fire, right? From what I am gathering from so many of you, *this* is happening.

Our shoes are off. We are low to the ground. We just said, "Here I am" (v. 4), and God is speaking. "So now, go. I am sending you to Pharaoh to bring my people the Israelites out of Egypt" (v. 10).

Ready for our response?

But Moses said to God, "Who am I that I should go to Pharaoh and bring the Israelites out of Egypt?"

That's what I would have said. You too?

Who am I? It's three questions really.

Who am I? This one is filled with absurd incredulity; as in, *There's no way you would be calling me to such a thing as this at such a time as this. I am no one. Unqualified. Not (fill in the blank) enough. Wrong number. Call someone else. I am out. It's a no.*

Who *am* I? This one is filled with implausible possibility; as in, *God must see something in me. I don't see it, but I am willing to look deeper. Is there a superhero suit in my closet I don't yet know about? Maybe there's more to me than anyone, including me, knows. I am leaning in. It's a definite maybe.*

Who am *I*? This one is filled with humble consideration; as in, *I'm clearly not qualified, but I did hear my name called . . . twice. The challenge is stratospherically beyond me, and yet I am not being asked for initiative but response. God, for whom nothing is impossible, is calling. This is not about me but him. I am willing. It's a yes.*

Real faith most often moves from no to maybe to yes. It's why God never stops sowing into people, and also why we must never stop. To God, no means not now—tell me more; maybe means definitely later—check back tomorrow; and yes means I've already ordered my uniform.

The truth? As we will see in the coming days, God is not so much asking us to do something as he is calling us to become someone; someone who is deeply surrendered to him, someone who trusts in the Lord with all their heart and leans not on their own understanding, who acknowledges him in all their ways so he can direct their paths (see Proverbs 3:5–6). That someone is who you most truly are in your deepest self, and so often, it's the someone (your false self) you've settled for that's in the way.

But Moses said to God, "Who am I that I should go to Pharaoh and bring the Israelites out of Egypt?"

So which version of "Who am I" is it for you?

The Prayer

Father, I want to be a person who says such things. Lead me along that path of faith—from no to maybe to yes; from incredulity to implausibility to irresistibility. I trust you and yet I know I hold back. There is more left in my surrender. I want to let go of anything false in me, that I might fully embrace who you have created me to become. Awaken me, Lord. Come, Holy Spirit, and train me to be such a person of faith. I pray in Jesus' name, amen.

The Questions

- Which version of "Who am I" is it for you? And in what ways have you settled for a lesser version of who you know God has called you to become?

. . . Understand the Obedience of Faith

40

EXODUS 3:12 | And God said, "I will be with you. And this will be the sign to you that it is I who have sent you: When you have brought the people out of Egypt, you will worship God on this mountain."

Consider This

Previously, at the unburning bush, God said to Moses, "So now, go. I am sending you to Pharaoh to bring my people the Israelites out of Egypt" (v. 10).

To which Moses replied, "Who am I that I should go to Pharaoh and bring the Israelites out of Egypt?" (v. 11).

Here may be the most beautiful and powerful part of the whole encounter. Behold God's answer to Moses' question:

"I will be with you."

God did not tell Moses why he was selected for the mission. He didn't say a single word about Moses' qualifications or lack thereof. God did not attempt to build up Moses' sense of self-worth or credibility or give him a pep talk or say, "You can do this, Moses!" The answer to "Who am I?" was:

"I will be with you."

In the face of impossible things and insurmountable challenges, God doesn't ask us to go and develop a strategic plan and then raise a gazillion dollars to make it happen. The truth? If it can be done with a strategic plan and a gazillion dollars, it's not big enough for God.

Get back in touch with the moment. The God of the cosmos made an appearance through an unburning bush on the far side of the wilderness to an octogenarian sheep herder and said he was sending him to rescue and deliver a nation of a million or more slaves from their oppressor, a man who happened to be the most powerful person in the world leading the most powerful nation on the planet.

I love how Timothy Tennent, my boss and the president of our seminary (and parent company), Asbury Theological Seminary, challenges me. He says we must attempt something so big that unless God intervenes it is destined to fail. And to all of our quandaries about impossible things and our quizzical inquiries about improbable outcomes, God responds with:

"I will be with you."

And he says the very same thing to you. It's fascinating to jump a thousand and five hundred or so years later to another unburning-bush moment on the mountain of God. This time it's the Son of God, our risen Lord, Jesus Christ, with eleven disciples in tow:

> Then Jesus came to them and said, "All authority in heaven and on earth has been given to me. Therefore go and make disciples of all nations, baptizing them in the name of the Father and of the Son and of the Holy Spirit, and teaching them to obey everything I have commanded you. And surely I am with you always, to the very end of the age." (Matt. 28:18–20)

It's like déjà vu, right? He said, "Go, I am sending you." They probably thought, *Who are we?* And he closed with, "I am with you."

So there's one more bit here. God gave Moses the sign of how he would know it was actually the God of heaven and earth who was sending him to do these impossible things.

"And this will be the sign to you that it is I who have sent you: When you have brought the people out of Egypt, you will worship God on this mountain."

"I will be with you," though a rock-solid promise, can seem a little touchy-feely at times. "You will worship God on this mountain" is a quite tangible, measurable, KPI (key performance indicator) kind of outcome. Still, here's the kicker: You receive the confirmation as a consequence of obedience to the vision. The sign comes after, not before. That's why we call it the obedience of faith.

Remember, though, it starts with a good old-fashioned, "Here I am!"

The Prayer

Father, I want to be a person who says such things. Here I am! Fill me with the fullness of Jesus. Here I am! Give me the audacity of Moses to have the guts to continue such a conversation with the Almighty. I claim the faith to trust a confirmation that comes after obedience rather than insisting on a sign as a precondition. Come, Holy Spirit, and train me to be such a person of faith. I pray in Jesus' name, amen.

The Questions

- How are you stirred by today's text and reflection? Do you sense the Spirit calling forth your audacity? Your obedience? Your faith? Are you declaring, "Here I am!"?

41 . . . Know Their Ontology

EXODUS 3:13–15 | Moses said to God, "Suppose I go to the Israelites and say to them, 'The God of your fathers has sent me to you,' and they ask me, 'What is his name?' Then what shall I tell them?"

God said to Moses, "I AM WHO I AM. This is what you are to say to the Israelites: 'I AM has sent me to you.'"

God also said to Moses, "Say to the Israelites, 'The LORD, the God of your fathers—the God of Abraham, the God of Isaac and the God of Jacob—has sent me to you.'

"This is my name forever,
the name you shall call me
from generation to generation."

Consider This

I am sometimes chided by my word choices in the Daily Text, especially by my dad. I am going to introduce a word today that may put me in hot water with him (and some of you). The word is *ontology*. Know what it means? To show that it is not an overly complicated word, I can change the "t" to a "c" and you will know exactly what that word means: oncology. It's a matter of practicality. Oncology, of course, is the study of cancer; something far too many of you know far too much about. It has gotten painfully practical in your life.

Ontology is a term from the field of metaphysics. More precisely, according to the *Oxford Dictionary*, ontology is "the philosophical study of the nature of being, becoming, existence, or reality." It's all the stuff we assume but never think about because our life is moving too fast to even consider it. Metaphysics is for a rainy day, but then it rains and we have a leak in the roof that must be fixed. If we had to name a subject for which the Bible is a textbook, it wouldn't be world religions. It would be ontology.

So why does this word matter today in the middle of what is now a weeklong encounter at a bush on fire but not burning up? Moses asks God the ontological question today:

Moses said to God, "Suppose I go to the Israelites and say to them, 'The God of your fathers has sent me to you,' and they ask me, 'What is his name?' Then what shall I tell them?"

Don't you love how Moses warms up to the idea of obeying God with, "Suppose I go . . ."? Moses wants to know with whom he deals here. Is this the Desert God or the Sun God or the Moon God or the Slave-Delivering God; which divine being is Moses engaging at this unburning bush? And God drops the ontological boom sauce:

God said to Moses, "I AM WHO I AM. This is what you are to say to the Israelites: 'I AM has sent me to you.'"

This is the ontological trump card: "I AM WHO I AM." It means something like, "I am God and there is no other. I am the ground of all being. There is no one like me. There is no equal to the being who precedes all beings."

God also said to Moses, "Say to the Israelites, 'The LORD, the God of your fathers—the God of Abraham, the God of Isaac and the God of Jacob—has sent me to you.'"

For whatever reason, this God of all gods—a.k.a. "I AM WHO I AM"—has chosen to make a covenant with this obscure family-become-nation and favored them above all other peoples, so that they might live as a sign of God's majestic and merciful glory for the sake of all other peoples. Now "I AM" is about to rescue them with a mighty hand and an outstretched arm.

So why does ontology matter? Here's how I see it. There are two modes of life: our existence and our being. There is how we exist in the world and who we are at the core. To the extent the core of our being is grounded in the ontological being of almighty God, who is "I AM," we will flourish in peace and prosperity irrespective of our circumstances. To the extent our core being is not grounded in the ontological being of almighty God, we will slavishly strive to maintain our existence, whether we be rich or poor, by any and all means available to us, turning to any and every god (including "I AM") we can conjure up who might help us.

God desires and delights to be with us in a comprehensive fashion, not as a peripheral help. He is looking for people who will say, "Have me!" rather than just pray, "Help me!"

He wants us to build our house on the rock rather than the sand, because the storms are coming. Is our core being flourishing in a grounded relationship with the one true and living God or are we just scraping out an existence the best we can?

So let me practically serve you as an ontologist today by asking you these questions:

Is the God and Father of our Lord Jesus Christ the core and central reality of your being and reality or do you turn to God only when you need help?

Are you increasingly abiding all the time in relationship with Jesus Christ or is he someone you once trusted for eternal salvation?

Do you depend on the fullness of the Holy Spirit to flourish in your daily life or are you hardly conscious of the Holy Spirit's presence and activity?

Why do I ask you such probing questions? "I AM" sent me.

The Prayer

Father, I want to be a person who says such things. I have so often and for so long turned to you as a transactional God for functional help. I need you when I need you and I don't when I don't. I am coming to the place where the center of gravity in my life must shift from me to you. You will be the ground of my being. Your life will become my life. Your love will become my love. Your power will become my power. Thank you, Jesus, for making me a disciple of yours rather than me constantly calling on you to run my errands. Come,

Holy Spirit, and train me to be such a person of faith. I pray in Jesus' name, amen.

The Question

- No further questions today, your honor.

42 . . . Don't Let Their Insufficiency Get in the Way of God's Calling

EXODUS 4:10–17 | Moses said to the Lord, "Pardon your servant, Lord. I have never been eloquent, neither in the past nor since you have spoken to your servant. I am slow of speech and tongue."

The Lord said to him, "Who gave human beings their mouths? Who makes them deaf or mute? Who gives them sight or makes them blind? Is it not I, the Lord? Now go; I will help you speak and will teach you what to say."

But Moses said, "Pardon your servant, Lord. Please send someone else."

Then the Lord's anger burned against Moses and he said, "What about your brother, Aaron the Levite? I know he can speak well. He is already on his way to meet you, and he will be glad to see you. You shall speak to him and put words in his mouth; I will help both of you speak and will teach you what to do. He will speak to the people for you, and it will be as if he were your mouth and as if you were God to him. But take this staff in your hand so you can perform the signs with it."

Consider This

Meanwhile back at the unburning bush, as the details unfold, Moses begins to see more reasons for why this might not be a good idea.

Moses said to the LORD, "Pardon your servant, Lord. I have never been eloquent, neither in the past nor since you have spoken to your servant. I am slow of speech and tongue."

What gave Moses the idea that God needed a silver-tongued preacher? Why is it that we tend to make the calling of God about our own qualifications or lack thereof? Do we think God is somehow not aware of our foibles, weaknesses, and incompetencies? What if God calls us into a particular assignment precisely because of our foibles, weaknesses, and incompetencies? What if God is looking for people who have been broken enough by life and mended enough by mercy that they know they are hopeless without God; that they can do nothing apart from Jesus? Isn't this the whole point of 2 Corinthians 4:7? "But we have this treasure in jars of clay to show that this all-surpassing power is from God and not from us."

Does Moses really think the secret sauce of his success in delivering the Israelites from the most powerful person on the planet is his eloquence of speech? Seems like Paul had something to say about eloquence now that I think about it:

> And so it was with me, brothers and sisters. When I came to you, I did not come with eloquence or human wisdom as I proclaimed to you the testimony about God. For I resolved to know nothing while I was with you except Jesus Christ and him crucified. I came to you in weakness with great fear and trembling. My message and my preaching were not with wise and persuasive words, but with a demonstration of the Spirit's power, so that your faith might not rest on human wisdom, but on God's power. (1 Cor. 2:1–5)

God does not need our talent, skills, or abilities to accomplish his will in the world. He can use them, but he doesn't need them. The only thing God needs from us is our availability, faithfulness, and teachability. God is good even in the face of our worst moments. Look how he responds to Moses:

"Now go; I will help you speak and will teach you what to say."

Indulge my translation in the form of an overused cliché: "God doesn't call the equipped. He equips the called." Still, after all God's patient coaxing, Moses (in what feels like his best British accent) says it's a hard pass:

But Moses said, "Pardon your servant, Lord. Please send someone else."

But, don't we see ourselves in good ole Moe? When it comes to the weighty matter of God's calling on our lives (and he calls us all), our insufficiency is a given. Now hear this: God's calling is about God's sufficiency, not our insufficiency. Okay, once again and this time with feeling: God's calling is about God's sufficiency, not our insufficiency.

The Prayer

Father, I want to be a person who says such things. Forgive me for making your calling about myself; for thinking you somehow need my gifts to accomplish your will or, worse, for thinking my lack of giftedness could somehow impede your work. Give me the grace to understand that when you call me you know what you are doing. Train my spirit to be available, faithful, and teachable. Come, Holy Spirit, and train me to be such a person of faith. I pray in Jesus' name, amen.

The Question

- Why do you tend to think you are not qualified enough or gifted enough or competent enough to respond to an invitation, assignment, or calling from God?

. . . Keep Ultimate Matters in View

43

EXODUS 4:18–23 | Then Moses went back to Jethro his father-in-law and said to him, "Let me return to my own people in Egypt to see if any of them are still alive."

Jethro said, "Go, and I wish you well."

Now the LORD had said to Moses in Midian, "Go back to Egypt, for all those who wanted to kill you are dead." So Moses took his wife and sons, put them on a donkey and started back to Egypt. And he took the staff of God in his hand.

The Lᴏʀᴅ said to Moses, "When you return to Egypt, see that you perform before Pharaoh all the wonders I have given you the power to do. But I will harden his heart so that he will not let the people go. Then say to Pharaoh, 'This is what the Lᴏʀᴅ says: Israel is my firstborn son, and I told you, "Let my son go, so he may worship me." But you refused to let him go; so I will kill your firstborn son.'"

Consider This

Penultimate—that's the word of the day. It means something like "secondary" or "second to the ultimate." And that's the problem. We get caught up in penultimate things to the point we lose sight of the ultimate thing.

We come to a moment where we need to get some altitude over our situation. We need to remember the big picture; to see beyond the penultimate to the ultimate. There is a critical word that has gotten lost in all of the conversation back and forth between Moses and God. We see it in verse 23 as God tells Moses what to say to Pharaoh:

"Let my son go, so he may worship me."

We saw it earlier when God told Moses the confirming sign of the whole affair would be that they would worship God on this mountain. Before it's all said and done, we will hear this refrain over and over and over again: "Let my people go, so that they may worship me."

"Let my people go" is penultimate; "so that they may worship me" is ultimate.

The penultimate purpose of deliverance is for the good of the people. The ultimate purpose of deliverance is for the glory of God. This is why worship matters so much. We were created to worship God. You and I and every other person on the face of planet Earth were made for one thing and one thing only: to worship the one true and living God—Father, Son, and Holy Spirit. We aren't worshipers because we worship. We worship because we are worshipers. Right up to the present moment, history shows us human beings will worship anything and everything under the sun, including the sun! In fact, the very essence of salvation and deliverance is to be rescued from the slavish oppression of a false god and brought into the gracious dominion of the true and living God.

We tend to think of worship as the thing we do (or used to do, as the case is these days) on Sunday at church. In fact, worship has pretty much been defined down to the act of singing to God. Hear me right—singing to God is worship, but it's only the tip of the tip of the iceberg.

To worship God is to orient one's entire being and life around the presence, purpose, and power of the God of heaven and earth, whom to know is to love. It is to live with an openhearted, single-minded, undivided love for God, his creation, and especially people. When we worship God, he brings our entire existence into the peace-filled, joyful life of love-governed power we were made for.

God knows our hearts will not rest until they rest in him; hence, his mission is to deliver us from our every unholy attachment, broken inclination, and involuntary bondage to worship false gods. We can think our mission is to do this good deed and give to that good cause and wrap it all up in religious garb and completely miss the point of the whole thing—more worshipers bringing more worship to God. As John Piper famously says, "Missions exists because worship doesn't." When we forget the ultimate thing, it's only a matter of time before the penultimate things become so much noise.

God does not deliver us so we can have a nice life in the suburbs with campfires and s'mores (and I do love me some s'mores). No, God saves, delivers, redeems, and blesses us so we can be burning bushes—on fire but not consumed—in our homes, neighborhoods, workplaces, churches, grocery stores, city centers, and places no one else dares to go.

Christian, you were meant for glory. You are made to be on fire for the God who made you. He made you to burn brightly for his glory and for your neighbor's good and for the deepest satisfaction you never imagined possible.

The Prayer

Father, I want to be a person who says such things. I confess I so easily get lost in the weeds of life, forgetting what it's all for and what it all means. I want to stop right now and open my heart to worship you; to stand in awe of you, even to kneel in humble reverence. Let my every waking minute take on that posture, in everything I am doing. Let the fiery glory of your love burn in me until all that is left is you; for then

I will truly be myself. Come, Holy Spirit, and train me to be such a person of faith. I pray in Jesus' name, amen.

The Questions
- Do you find yourself caught up in penultimate matters? Are you needing to be reset for ultimate matters? Will you find a quiet place, a closet, somewhere you can open up your adoration to the God and Father of our Lord Jesus Christ? And don't forget to say, "Here I am!"

. . . Believe God Has a Plan

44

PSALM 106:6–13 | We have sinned, even as our ancestors did;
  we have done wrong and acted wickedly.
When our ancestors were in Egypt,
they gave no thought to your miracles;
  they did not remember your many kindnesses,
  and they rebelled by the sea, the Red Sea.
Yet he saved them for his name's sake,
  to make his mighty power known.
He rebuked the Red Sea, and it dried up;
  he led them through the depths as through a desert.
He saved them from the hand of the foe;
  from the hand of the enemy he redeemed them.

The waters covered their adversaries;
>   not one of them survived.
Then they believed his promises
>   and sang his praise.

But they soon forgot what he had done
>   and did not wait for his plan to unfold.

Consider This

There's an insight coming to me as we walk our way toward Egypt. It's coming with the slow-building intensity of a snowball rolling down a hill, getting larger with each turn. As usual, it's an obvious insight; me being the master of the obvious insight and all. You ready for it? Here it is: God has a plan.

It's not a general plan with lots of gaps that people need to fill in with their best ideas and ingenuity. The plan certainly involves people, but it's a particular plan. Think back with me just a bit to the book of Exodus. From the start, God sees the particularity of the suffering of the Israelites and he meets it with the particularity of a solution.

In 3:17, he spoke of not just getting them out of Egypt, but taking them to "a land flowing with milk and honey."

In 3:18, God instructed Moses to go first to the elders of Israel and share the plan with them. And after that they were to go to Pharaoh.

In 3:19, God let Moses know on the front end that though the elders of Israel will favor and follow him, Pharaoh will not. It will take "a mighty hand" and a series of great signs and wonders.

In 3:21, God let Moses know that before it is all over, the Egyptian people will pour out great favor on the Israelites in their exodus. Look at the exquisite detail God gave Moses about his strategic plan in their very first encounter:

> "Every woman is to ask her neighbor and any woman living in her house for articles of silver and gold and for clothing, which you will put on your sons and daughters. And so you will plunder the Egyptians." (3:22)

Here's what I marvel at. Moses didn't come up with any of this. None of it was his idea. From soup to nuts, this was God's plan. The purpose was worship. The vision was a land flowing with milk and honey. The mission was "Let my people go." The strategy was signs and wonders. The ten plagues, the Passover, the Red Sea, every last bit of this was God's plan. All God needed was faithful, available, teachable, obedient, moderately competent people to follow directions.

In this day and age, we have mastered the art of making plans and carrying them out. We might pray and ask God to help our planning or inspire our plans. We are experts at asking God to bless our plans. It all has me wondering what it would be like to spend more time on the front end simply asking God for his plan. It requires a lot more deference, submission, humility, and waiting than comes natural to me.

It makes me realize just how ready I am to assume that my plan is God's plan. I prefer to couch my impatience and lack of faith in the clothing of taking initiative.

The last verse in today's text captured my attention:

But they soon forgot what he had done and did not wait for his plan to unfold.

The psalmist was referring to the Israelites and the exodus. This was after God executed his masterful plan and delivered them from Egypt and through the Red Sea.

I wonder if it might be the perfect opportunity to start our days asking God for his plan. And waiting for it.

The Prayer

Father, I want to be a person who says such things. If I'm honest, I am just like the Israelites. I need to be infused with a humility I know not. I'm reaching for a better way, far less self-dependent (or independent, as the case may be) and far more dependent; far more submissive; far more willing to wait for your plan to unfold. No one has proven themselves more faithful to fulfill their plan than you. Come, Holy Spirit, and train me to be such a person of faith. I pray in Jesus' name, amen.

The Questions

- Do you tend to think God expects us to come up with the plan and then ask him to bless it? Do you, like me, prefer to take initiative rather than to wait on God?

. . . Know They Can't Go This Way Alone

45

EXODUS 4:14–17 | Then the LORD's anger burned against Moses and he said, "What about your brother, Aaron the Levite? I know he can speak well. He is already on his way to meet you, and he will be glad to see you. You shall speak to him and put words in his mouth; I will help both of you speak and will teach you what to do. He will speak to the people for you, and it will be as if he were your mouth and as if you were God to him. But take this staff in your hand so you can perform the signs with it."

Consider This

Did you realize Moses never actually said yes to God? He politely declined in verse 13, and then we get today's text. Moses never responded positively. You know who did? Aaron. Aaron said yes, and Moses joined him. The next thing we hear is this: "Then Moses went back to Jethro his father-in-law and said to him, 'Let me return to my own people in Egypt to see if any of them are still alive'" (v. 18).

Moses did not lead. He followed Aaron. In truth, they followed each other in their pursuit of the God who called them. That's how it works in God's kingdom. In a kingdom friendship, there is no hero because they keep trading the lead. Each hides himself in the other.

It wasn't God's calling that elicited Moses' yes. It was Aaron's obedience to God. The only thing more daunting in answering an assignment from God is the thought of doing it alone. And the truth? God never intends for us to go at it alone. He wants us banded together with brothers and sisters, sharing in the bonded fellowship of the Holy Spirit, encouraging one another, blessing one another, speaking grace and truth to one another, calling out the best in one another, bearing one another's burdens, and so fulfilling the law of Christ. In summary, he wants us banded together in ways where we can learn to actually become the love of God for each other. And when we become the love of God for one another, it changes the world.

As God chose the brothers, Moses and Aaron, Jesus chose two sets of brothers as his first four disciples. Peter and Andrew and James and John. I think of David and Jonathan, Ruth and Naomi, Paul and Barnabas, Mary and Elizabeth; all exemplars of the way God prefers banded friendships to lone rangers. And who would the Lone Ranger have been without his trusted Tonto? From Frodo and Sam in *The Lord of the Rings* to Napoleon and Pedro in *Napoleon Dynamite* to Butch Cassidy and Sundance to Thelma and Louise—all the great stories are stories of banded friendships.

> The LORD said to Aaron, "Go into the wilderness to meet Moses." So he met Moses at the mountain of God and kissed him. Then Moses told Aaron everything the LORD had sent him to say, and also about all the signs he had commanded him to perform. (vv. 27–28)

Imagine the excited relief of the both of them as they stood there at the mountain of God in a brotherly embrace, comparing notes of their respective God stories. They were doing the stuff—together!

Sadly, this is not so common in today's world. Most of us suffer from the syndrome: "Too many acquaintances; not enough friends." We find ourselves in community groups and Bible studies, yet hungering for the deeper bonds that characterize the band of Jesus.

Two things he said that live together at the core of my being. They are my passion:

> "Very truly I tell you, whoever believes in me will do the works I have been doing, and they will do even greater things than these, because I am going to the Father." (John 14:12)

> "Greater love has no one than this: to lay down one's life for one's friends." (John 15:13)

I am 100-percent convinced we will see the greater things from the disciples of Jesus when we see the greater love among the friends of Jesus.

I'm not talking about BFFs or Christian cliques or holy huddles. It is banded discipleship—simultaneously the most transformational and missional thing we can do, and it's the secret sauce of great awakening.

"I no longer call you servants," Jesus said, "Instead I have called you friends" (see John 15:15). I am coming to the crystallized conviction that you can't be a friend of Jesus unless you are a friend of the friends of Jesus.

The Prayer

Father, I want to be a person who says such things. I want be a friend of the friends of Jesus. I don't want to just be a sheep that gets fed. I want to obey the command of Jesus to feed his sheep. I don't know how or who or anything else really, but I know I want more of Jesus in my life and I am becoming convinced I can only find that in the deeper bonds of banded discipleship. Come, Holy Spirit, and train me to be such a person of faith. I pray in Jesus' name, amen.

The Questions

- Do you have any kingdom friends? Are you ready to at least explore the realm of banded discipleship?

46 . . . Know Deliverance Is Costly

EXODUS 5:1–5 | Afterward Moses and Aaron went to Pharaoh and said, "This is what the Lord, the God of Israel, says: 'Let my people go, so that they may hold a festival to me in the wilderness.'"

Pharaoh said, "Who is the Lord, that I should obey him and let Israel go? I do not know the Lord and I will not let Israel go."

Then they said, "The God of the Hebrews has met with us. Now let us take a three-day journey into the wilderness to offer sacrifices to the Lord our God, or he may strike us with plagues or with the sword."

But the king of Egypt said, "Moses and Aaron, why are you taking the people away from their labor? Get back to your work!" Then Pharaoh said, "Look, the people of the land are now numerous, and you are stopping them from working."

Consider This

Moses and Aaron must have thought to themselves, *This will only take a couple of days.* They were obeying God, moving in his grant of authority. They had received the favor of the elders of Israel. A couple of conversations with Pharaoh should do the trick. After all, they were doing the will of God, right?

"If God is for us, who can be against us" (Rom. 8:31), right? Short answer: Pharaoh can be against us. Though God must win the battle, it doesn't mean there will not be a ton of opposition, struggle, hardship, and loss along the way. There is an interpretive heading over chapter 5 in most of our Bibles. Three words tell the story: "Bricks Without Straw."

> That same day Pharaoh gave this order to the slave drivers and overseers in charge of the people: "You are no longer to supply the people with straw for making bricks; let them go and gather their own straw. But require them to make the same number of bricks as before; don't reduce the quota. They are lazy;

that is why they are crying out, 'Let us go and sacrifice to our God.' Make the work harder for the people so that they keep working and pay no attention to lies." (Ex. 5:6–9)

In the matter of deliverance, the bricks-without-straw principle teaches us things will often get worse before they get better. I hate to say it, but I think this is par for the course. The will of God diametrically opposes the will of Satan. The forces of evil, the powers, principalities, rulers, and authorities of this present darkness will not release their hold without a fight. Pharaoh will not willingly give up his slave labor force. They are building his kingdom.

Moses returned to the Lord and said, "Why, Lord, why have you brought trouble on this people? Is this why you sent me? Ever since I went to Pharaoh to speak in your name, he has brought trouble on this people, and you have not rescued your people at all." (Ex. 5:22–23)

Pursuing the will of God will not mean smooth sailing. It does not mean life will get easier. It will be better, but likely harder. You can expect tremendous blessing and yet you can be guaranteed significant struggle and difficulty. Though many others will be blessed, even future generations to come, the people around and associated with you will often pay a price or suffer a consequence for your obedience.

Deliverance is costly. Ask Jesus. It's why he says things to us like, "Whoever wants to be my disciple must deny themselves and take up their cross daily and follow me" (Luke 9:23). Ask

Moses and Aaron. As glorious as the outcome will be, the process can be excruciating and the work often thankless:

> The Israelite overseers realized they were in trouble when they were told, "You are not to reduce the number of bricks required of you for each day." When they left Pharaoh, they found Moses and Aaron waiting to meet them, and they said, "May the LORD look on you and judge you! You have made us obnoxious to Pharaoh and his officials and have put a sword in their hand to kill us." (Ex. 5:19–21)

Moses and Aaron carried the cross before there was a cross. Or did they? God reveals a great mystery to us through the lives and obedience of Moses and Aaron. It is this: there was never a time before the cross. Why do I say this? Because the cross is the love of God—a never-ending love. Revelation 13:8 reminds us the Lamb was slain from before the foundation of the world.

The Prayer

Father, I want to be a person who says such things. I marvel at who you are. From before time and the world came to be, you are self-giving love. You give yourself away. You love in such costly ways. And this is what you will for me: to love in costly ways, to lay down my life for my friends, to give myself away. And you will do it in and through me. Come, Holy Spirit, and train me to be such a person of faith. I pray in Jesus' name, amen.

The Questions

- Are you grasping more of the mystery of the profundity and power of the love of God? You know what he does for you. Are you ready for him to do more in you and then through you?

47 ... Trust in God's Word over Their Experience

EXODUS 6:1–8 | Then the Lord said to Moses, "Now you will see what I will do to Pharaoh: Because of my mighty hand he will let them go; because of my mighty hand he will drive them out of his country."

God also said to Moses, "I am the Lord. I appeared to Abraham, to Isaac and to Jacob as God Almighty, but by my name the Lord I did not make myself fully known to them. I also established my covenant with them to give them the land of Canaan, where they resided as foreigners. Moreover, I have heard the groaning of the Israelites, whom the Egyptians are enslaving, and I have remembered my covenant.

"Therefore, say to the Israelites: 'I am the Lord, and I will bring you out from under the yoke of the Egyptians. I will free you from being slaves to them, and I will redeem you with an outstretched arm and with mighty acts of judgment. I will take you as my own people, and I will be your God. Then you will know that I am the Lord your God, who brought you out from under the yoke of the Egyptians. And I will bring you to the land I swore with uplifted hand to give to Abraham, to Isaac and to Jacob. I will give it to you as a possession. I am the Lord.'"

Consider This

Will we trust the Word of God or defer to the experience of people?

The Word of God is powerful. We believe it. These eight verses from Exodus today are packed with powerful declarations from the mouth of God. Seventeen times he says some form of I am or I will. Here's the highlight reel: "I am the Lord. I appeared. I also established. I have heard. I have remembered. I will bring you out. I will free you. I will redeem you. I will take you as my own people. I will be your God. I will bring you to the land. I will give it to you as a possession. I am the Lord."

This is nothing short of incredible. It would be more difficult to be more reassured by the Word of God than one would be in this instance.

The truth is we never hear the Word of God in a vacuum. We almost always hear it in the light of our own experience; our experience of life, the world, sin, death, brokenness, betrayal, failure, success, trauma, pain, deception, disappointment, our strengths, our weaknesses, our Meyers-Briggs personality type, our enneagram number, our horoscope, and a thousand other things.

In light of their slavery and most recent episode of making bricks without straw, the Israelites, including

Moses, allowed their experience to override their faith in the Word of God: "Moses reported this to the Israelites, but they did not listen to him because of their discouragement and harsh labor" (v. 9).

Though the power of the Word of God is to the power of our experience as the power of the sun is to that of the moon, somehow our experience manages to tip the scale all too often. The Israelites' powerful experience of "discouragement and harsh labor," though clearly inferior to the power of God's Word, overcame their confidence in the Word of God: "Then the LORD said to Moses, 'Go, tell Pharaoh king of Egypt to let the Israelites go out of his country'" (vv. 10–11).

The experience of early failure in the mission also tipped the scale on Moses' confidence in God's Word. He regressed all the way back to his faltering speech excuse: "But Moses said to the LORD, 'If the Israelites will not listen to me, why would Pharaoh listen to me, since I speak with faltering lips?'" (v. 12).

The Word of God is just that, the Word of God. Our experience as human beings is just that, our experience. The thing that tells the difference is the quality of our faith. Will we offer faith in the face of our faltering experience? Will we trust God's Word anyway? The tumor is malignant and the cancer has spread. The marriage is irreconcilable. Your son or daughter has forayed into a socially affirmed yet biblically forbidden lifestyle. Will we place our faith in the Word of God or defer to our experience and that of others?

And the next thing you know, we are taking a commercial break for something completely different, a fourteen-verse genealogical diversion (see Exodus 6:13–27).

Faith in the Word of God leads to another kind of experience. Given time and patient trust, faith in the Word of God leads to the indelible, life-changing experience of the faithfulness of God to the promise of his Word. All of this will form the curriculum for the people of God for the next forty years:

> Now faith is confidence in what we hope for and assurance about what we do not see. This is what the ancients were commended for. (Heb. 11:1–2)

The Prayer

Father, I want to be a person who says such things. The old hymn comes to mind:

'Tis so sweet to trust in Jesus,
and to take him at his word;
just to rest upon his promise,
and to know, "Thus saith the Lord."

Jesus, Jesus, how I trust him!
How I've proved you o'er and o'er.
Jesus, Jesus, precious Jesus!
O for grace to trust him more!*

---

* Louisa M. R. Stead, "'Tis So Sweet to Trust in Jesus," 1882, public domain.

That about says it all for me today, Lord. Come, Holy Spirit, and train me to be such a person of faith. I pray in Jesus' name, amen.

The Questions

- What is it that most convinces you that your experience or that of another should be trusted over and above the Word of God? How do you see this struggle in your own life? How are you doing with it?

48 . . . Keep a Soft Heart in God's Hands

EXODUS 7:1–7 | Then the Lord said to Moses, "See, I have made you like God to Pharaoh, and your brother Aaron will be your prophet. You are to say everything I command you, and your brother Aaron is to tell Pharaoh to let the Israelites go out of his country. But I will harden Pharaoh's heart, and though I multiply my signs and wonders in Egypt, he will not listen to you. Then I will lay my hand on Egypt and with mighty acts of judgment I will bring out my divisions, my people the Israelites. And the Egyptians will know that I am the Lord when I stretch out my hand against Egypt and bring the Israelites out of it."

Moses and Aaron did just as the Lord commanded them. Moses was eighty years old and Aaron eighty-three when they spoke to Pharaoh.

Consider This

We come today to what we might call a "sticky wicket." I can't explain it; hence I want to avoid it, but it must be dealt with. It comes in verse 3 as follows: *But I will harden Pharaoh's heart.*

How is it fair if God punishes Pharaoh for something God does to Pharaoh? In other words, how is Pharaoh responsible for a condition God brought upon him? I can't explain it. I will point out the following though.

Ten times we see this reference to God hardening Pharaoh's heart (see Exodus 4:21; 7:3; 9:12; 10:1, 20, 27; 11:10; 14:4, 8, 17). Here's the interesting part. Ten times we see references to Pharaoh hardening his own heart (see Exodus 7:13, 14, 22; 8:15, 19, 32; 9:7, 34, 35; 13:15). Can we call it a tie?

Does God predestine every outcome to the nth detail or does God allow human beings the free will and agency to make their own choices? Just like this tie, the debate between predestination and free will is utterly unresolvable. Depending on which side people take, they can marshal the evidence either way. Though I believe the predestinarians are wrong, as a lawyer, I will grant they can make a straight-faced case before the judge.

I am not a predestinarian. I believe God gives people free will and holds them responsible for their choices. Having debated it exhaustively (and exhaustingly) I am also thoroughly uninterested in debating the unresolvable issue any further. I have died on that hill too many times.

In the present case, I look to Pharaoh's very first response to the Word of God. Pharaoh said, "Who is the LORD, that I should obey him and let Israel go? I do not know the LORD and I will not let Israel go" (Ex. 5:2). Pharaoh shows us a hard heart from the start. To say that God allows a person to harden their heart to the point of thwarting his word and will does not mean that God hardened their heart. It means God allows people to go their own way and, in the end, to suffer the consequences.

When hard-hearted people go their own way, it creates enormous hardship and suffering for many others. To agree that God willed Pharaoh's hardened heart is necessarily to agree that God also willed all of the consequent destruction and losses to many people who were not themselves culpable. To attribute responsibility to Pharaoh for his own hardness of heart means he is also responsible for the far-reaching consequences his ill will wrought on the nation.

Bottom line: to say God hardened Pharaoh's heart, in my judgment, means God allowed Pharaoh to harden his own heart. Said another way, God gave Pharaoh over to the hardness of his own heart. Pharaoh was given at least ten chances to reverse course, to repent, and relent from his rebellion. I see the same general principle operative in Romans 1:24–25, which says:

> Therefore God gave them over in the sinful desires of their hearts to sexual impurity for the degrading of their bodies with one another. They exchanged the truth about God for a lie, and worshiped and served created things rather than the Creator—who is forever praised. Amen.

One final exhibit: after all the extraordinary deliverance and advantage he would give the Israelites, God would allow his own people to harden their hearts against him. Psalm 95:7b–10 recounts the story for all the future generations to come—especially ours:

> Today, if only you would hear his voice,
> "Do not harden your hearts as you did at Meribah,
>   as you did that day at Massah in the wilderness,
> where your ancestors tested me;
>   they tried me, though they had seen what I did.
> For forty years I was angry with that generation;
>   I said, 'They are a people whose hearts go astray,
>   and they have not known my ways.'"

He wants our hearts, friends, our soft, pliable, clay-like hearts in his hands, where he can mold them, by the power of the Word and the Spirit, into vessels of his liking, for his purposes, for our good and his glory. It's why his wisdom beckons to us, "Trust in the LORD with all your heart and lean not on your own understanding; in all your ways submit to him, and he will make your paths straight" (Prov. 3:5–6).

The Prayer

Father, I want to be a person who says such things. I give you my heart. Break through the outer hardness and heal inner hardness, and restore the fullness of your image in me. I trust you yet I want to trust you more. Teach me to hear your voice, even your whisper. Come, Holy Spirit, and train me to be such a person of faith. I pray in Jesus' name, amen.

The Questions

- How do you relate to this reflection on the issue of God hardening Pharaoh's heart and Pharaoh hardening his own heart? But before you answer that question, what is the state of your own heart?

49 . . . Repent Rather than Readjust

EXODUS 8:15 | But when Pharaoh saw that there was relief, he hardened his heart and would not listen to Moses and Aaron, just as the Lord had said.

Consider This

We come now to the dreaded plagues and, of all times to come, they choose to come now, in the midst of a global plague. I mean pandemic.*

---

* After considering whether or not to leave the current event references to COVID-19 in the published book version of the online Daily Text, I have decided to leave it. This could, in fact, date the book, yet I am good with this outcome. The timing of the extraordinary pandemic of 2020 and the ways it coincided with this series were uncanny. The global pandemic, while not akin to the biblical plagues, merits a long remembrance and a deep wrestling that may well transcend our time.

I don't see COVID-19 as a plague sent by God to punish people or send a prophetic message or anything like that. COVID-19 is epidemiology 101. It is basic cause-and-effect. Germs spread and they cause disease. Still, people want to know if God sent this particular disease, or rather allowed it, in order to send some kind of message. Unless maybe the message is to wash your hands more, I don't see it that way. Does God send the flu every year in order to make a point? Surely not.

It is another question to ask what God might be up to in the midst of such a global crisis. It comes back to something I have said before in the Daily Text: everything that happens is not God's will, but God has a will in everything that happens. Here are some ways we might inquire of the Lord with respect to COVID-19: "Father, what might you be up to in the midst of this global crisis? What might you be saying to your people (a.k.a. the church) through these days of disruption? How might you be leading us to respond to our neighbors, especially those who may be far from you? How might you be awakening us from sleep in this moment in history? Lord Jesus, how might we sow with you for awakening in the days ahead?"

As I ponder these ten plagues, which occur between chapters 7 and 11, there's an observation I would like to test with you. I observe a behavioral phenomenon with Pharaoh's response to the plagues that I believe illuminates a broken pattern in human nature in the midst of a crisis situation. Here's the pattern: Plague comes. Pharaoh agrees to relent and release the Israelites. Plague stops. Pharaoh reverts back to his former recalcitrance. Rinse and Repeat.

Here is an example of what I reference:

> Then Pharaoh summoned Moses and Aaron. "This time I have sinned," he said to them. "The Lord is in the right, and I and my people are in the wrong. Pray to the Lord, for we have had enough thunder and hail. I will let you go; you don't have to stay any longer." (Ex. 9:27–28)

Watch what happens next: "When Pharaoh saw that the rain and hail and thunder had stopped, he sinned again: He and his officials hardened their hearts" (Ex. 9:34).

It's tempting to characterize Pharaoh's response as a change of heart. It even appears to be confession and repentance. Once the plague relents, though, he reverts back to his former posture. He has not changed at all. He merely responded to a crisis in what seemed to him as an expedient solution.

After each plague we see the same pattern. What if this is the definition of hard-heartedness—the refusal to see repentance through to real results? A hard-hearted person will respond to disaster just like everyone else. They want relief. The difference is a hard-hearted person will not ultimately change. They simply readjust.

When they go back to their old normal, it creates a new normal for everyone else. Because of my refusal to change, other people are forced to adjust to the conditions created by my hard heart. Note how costly Pharaoh's hard-heartedness proves for the people of Egypt. It will result in enormous losses, the chief of which will be the death of the firstborn son in every single household.

This present plague of a pandemic will pass. From horrific terror strikes to mass shootings, they always do. The question is: Will we change and seamlessly shift into the new normal or will we attune our lives to the ways God may be calling us to repent and realign with his kingdom going forward?

I guess the question I am asking has to do with awakening. Sometimes we confuse waking up with hitting the snooze bar. The alarm of crisis goes off and it registers, yet we all too easily hit the snooze bar for another nine minutes of sleep. We sort of woke up, but not really. I'm afraid that's how it is with these situations like we find ourselves in now. The alarm can be deafening and yet we somehow find a way to hit snooze until the next one. What if the matter of hard-heartedness is not as simple as comparing oneself to the obvious example of an ancient abusive Pharaoh? What if the more subtle symptom of hard-heartedness is waking up just enough to push the snooze bar and then back to the slumber of the old normal?

We've been through this enough now to know it is likely to happen again. How many new normals must we adjust to before saying enough? If we don't do something different this time we will slowly adjust to the new normal, stocking our homes with the right kind of protective masks along with a six-month supply of toilet paper. The sports and enter- tainment engines will kick back into high gear. We will sing our favorite songs a bit louder at church. The stock market will rise again. We will salute our health-care professionals and drift back into our bad habits. I'm not being cynical—just honest. We've seen it happen too many times now to think anything will change unless we actually change in a sustained way.

So what can be different this time going forward? I have an idea. It involves a much deeper bonded attachment in the Holy Spirit between ordinary Christians. We need a great awakening. Neither the old normal nor the new normal will bring us any closer. It is going to take making new room in our lives for a few more people.

The Prayer

Father, I want to be a person who says such things. I confess I have been a part of the problem in the ways I have allowed myself to adjust to too many new normals. I want to say enough, yet I don't want to shout it at the world in anger but to say it to myself. I know I must change and yet I know my will to change is not enough. It will take making some new room in my life, different than I know now. Come, Holy Spirit, and train me to be such a person of faith. I pray in Jesus' name, amen.

The Questions

- Are you seeing and sensing what I am sensing about such moments as these? Are you open to exploring the hardness of your own heart? Isn't that what the ever-progressing new normals do to us—harden our hearts?

. . . Revel in the Grace of the Gospel

EXODUS 11:6–7 | "'There will be loud wailing throughout Egypt—worse than there has ever been or ever will be again. But among the Israelites not a dog will bark at any person or animal.' Then you will know that the LORD makes a distinction between Egypt and Israel."

Consider This

The concept of judgment, unpopular as it may be with many, is a monumental reality in Scripture and the Christian faith. There is something within all of us that both wants to judge but does not want to be judged. And, let's be honest, the effect of judgment is discrimination, which is the absolute anathema of our age.

In the matter at hand, God clearly discriminates between the Israelites and the Egyptians. He judges the Israelites favorably while condemning the Egyptians:

> Then Moses summoned all the elders of Israel and said to them, "Go at once and select the animals for your families and slaughter the Passover lamb. Take a bunch of hyssop, dip it into the blood in the basin and put some of the blood on the top and on both sides of the doorframe. None of you shall go out of the door of your house until morning. When the LORD goes through the land to strike down the Egyptians,

> he will see the blood on the top and sides of the door-frame and will pass over that doorway, and he will not permit the destroyer to enter your houses and strike you down." (Ex. 12:21–23)

Here's what I think about: What if an Egyptian had put the blood of a lamb over their own doorframe? What would have happened? My hunch: they would have been spared. Why? Because the judgment of God comes down to one thing—the blood of the Lamb. A person is covered by the blood of the Lamb or they are not. It really is that simple.

It is an astonishing thing to think about Jesus and his final Passover meal and his earthshaking claim with the bread and the cup; that it was his very body and his blood. He is our Passover, but this Passover is not restricted to the Jewish people. This Passover is for everyone. Judgment is coming upon the whole earth. Mercy is freely available in Jesus Christ. We are saved by his blood shed on the cross. He is the Lamb of God who takes away the sins of the world. This is the gospel of God.

I struggle to grasp how it is somehow unfair and discriminatory that eternal salvation and entrance into the kingdom of God is offered freely and inclusively to the entire human race exclusively through the life, death, and resurrection of Jesus Christ. Though many refuse to believe, no one is excluded. It is all at once the most exclusive and inclusive offer imaginable. Why is this unfair? The human race, for all our good qualities, is utterly wicked and totally depraved. No one is righteous, not even one (see Romans 3:10). No one deserves the grace and mercy of God. God owes salvation to no one. It is the free gift of grace to all who would believe and receive. Like the ancient Israelites, when we trust in the blood of the Lamb, we are delivered from slavery and set free to live the life for which we were created.

In the end, it is judgment to be sure, but judgment crowned with mercy. Read these next words very deliberately and carefully. Everything, literally everything, we believe is anchored in these revealed words:

> All this is from God, who reconciled us to himself through Christ and gave us the ministry of reconciliation: that God was reconciling the world to himself in Christ, not counting people's sins against them. And he has committed to us the message of reconciliation. We are therefore Christ's ambassadors, as though God were making his appeal through us. We implore you on Christ's behalf: Be reconciled to God. God made him who had no sin to be sin for us, so that in him we might become the righteousness of God. (2 Cor. 5:18–21)

The Prayer

Father, I want to be a person who says such things. Thank you for the gospel of Jesus Christ, our Passover Lamb, who takes away the sins of the world. Help me to understand and so deeply internalize this message that I am compelled and even constrained to be an ambassador of this merciful reconciliation. I know it is foolishness to those who are perishing, but let that not stop me from sharing it anyway. Come, Holy Spirit, and train me to be such a person of faith. I pray in Jesus' name, amen.

The Questions

- Do you struggle with the exclusive message of the gospel? If so, why does it seem unfair to you? If you had terminal cancer and there was only one cure, would you be offended at that? What is the difference?

51 . . . Watch and Pray

EXODUS 12:37–42 ESV | And the people of Israel journeyed from Rameses to Succoth, about six hundred thousand men on foot, besides women and children. A mixed multitude also went up with them, and very much livestock, both flocks and herds. And they baked unleavened cakes of the dough that they had brought out of Egypt, for it was not leavened, because they were thrust out of Egypt and could not wait, nor had they prepared any provisions for themselves.

The time that the people of Israel lived in Egypt was 430 years. At the end of 430 years, on that very day, all the hosts of the Lord went out from the land of Egypt. It was a night of watching by the Lord, to bring them out of the land of Egypt; so this same night is a night of watching kept to the Lord by all the people of Israel throughout their generations.

Consider This

Four hundred thirty years. Get your mind around that. For those of us who live in the United States, we have only been a country for 244 years. I don't have a calculation for how many of those 430 years the Israelites spent enslaved, but it was likely most of them. In other words, no one's great-great-great-grandfather who was already long dead likely remembered a time when slavery was not the norm. Just as freedom rings in the deepest sense of our identity as Americans, slavery rang in the deepest sense of the Israelites' core identity.

Other than some prevenient whisper of freedom resident in their deepest DNA as human beings, they had utterly no concept of anything else but slavery. There were no Ten Commandments yet, no tabernacle, no sacrificial system to speak of, no priests, Levites, or anything of the sort. There was the aging memory of Abraham, Isaac, and Jacob. They did have one thing going for them: I Am was with them. The God of Abraham, Isaac, and Jacob was for them.

Six hundred thousand men plus women and children and livestock—conservatively, two million people. Get your mind around that. As a point of reference, that is roughly the population of Houston, Texas. They have just been through ten successive plagues of absolute cataclysmic proportion. They are on foot walking out of the country en route to the promised land. It would take forty years to get there. They would get out of Egypt overnight. It would take another forty years to get Egypt out of them.

Here's a marvel. Despite centuries of captivity, from generation to generation to generation, the Israelites never stopped crying out to God. They kept their watch. They never gave up:

> Then the LORD said, "I have surely seen the affliction of my people who are in Egypt and have heard their cry because of their taskmasters. I know their sufferings, and I have come down to deliver them out of the hand of the Egyptians and to bring them up out of that land to a good and broad land, a land flowing with milk and honey, to the place of the Canaanites, the Hittites, the Amorites, the Perizzites, the Hivites, and the Jebusites. And now, behold, the cry of the people of Israel has come to me, and I have also seen the oppression with which the Egyptians oppress them." (Ex. 3:7–9 ESV)

While I don't believe God is waiting for a threshold count of numbers of people or years of duration praying before he responds, there is something about a slow-growing wave of prayer over a long period of time that, historically speaking, precedes awakenings. There is no formula, just deep, sustained yearning that can only come from a real, deep place of travail.

Here's what most amazes me about today's text. Referencing the night of the exodus from Egypt, we read:

It was a night of watching by the LORD, to bring them out of the land of Egypt . . .

A night of watching by the LORD.

Get your mind around that. Their eyes were on God. God's eyes were on them. When the watchfulness of the people meets up with the watchfulness of the Lord, the miracle happens.

Then comes this final word from the text:

. . . so this same night is a night of watching kept to the Lord by all the people of Israel throughout their generations.

There are so many stories I want to share at this moment. Only one seems necessary. Twenty-one years ago I received a calling within my calling. It is one I have both succeeded and failed to fulfill. This calling came to me one morning with the clarity of a winter sunrise. It emerged from a word of Scripture: "Devote yourselves to prayer, being watchful and thankful" (Col. 4:2). The Lord impressed upon me these words: "Create space for prayer." From that day forward, I have stumbled and fallen and stumbled again, and yet I keep getting back up.

I believe I am hearing from the Lord that the day of march has come again. I believe it is time to embark on a movement of 24-7 prayer in our work to sow for a great awakening. As I see the words unfold on my screen it feels both overwhelming and right:

> Devote yourselves to prayer, being watchful and thankful. (Col. 4:2)

The Prayer

Father, I want to be a person who says such things. My vision is clouded by so many things, even good things, and yet distractions from the only necessary thing Jesus taught us. Thank you that your watch is upon me, Lord. Train me to set my watch upon you. I long to fix my gaze upon you, Jesus, to keep watch with you, to come to the place where my watch meets your watch. Come, Holy Spirit, and train me to be such a person of faith. I pray in Jesus' name, amen.

The Questions

- What holds you back from an undivided heart of watchfulness and prayer? What do you have to lose? What might there be to gain?

52 ... Know the Whole Story

EXODUS 13:3–10 | Then Moses said to the people, "Commemorate this day, the day you came out of Egypt, out of the land of slavery, because the LORD brought you out of it with a mighty hand. Eat nothing containing yeast. Today, in the month of Aviv, you are leaving. When the LORD brings you into the land of the Canaanites, Hittites, Amorites, Hivites and Jebusites—the land he swore to your ancestors to give you, a land flowing with milk and honey—you are to observe this ceremony in this month: For seven days eat bread made without yeast and on the seventh day hold a festival to the LORD. Eat unleavened bread during those seven days; nothing with yeast in it is to be seen among you, nor shall any yeast be seen anywhere within your borders. On that day tell your son, 'I do this because of what the Lord did for me when I came out of Egypt.' This observance will be for you like a sign on your hand and a reminder on your forehead that this law of the Lord is to be on your lips. For the Lord brought you out of Egypt with his mighty hand. You must keep this ordinance at the appointed time year after year."

Consider This

If I asked you to tell me your story, chances are you wouldn't include the Passover and exodus story. I probably wouldn't either. Why is this?

If you asked me to tell you my story, I couldn't tell it without talking about Jesus and the resurrection. Same for you, right?

The question, though, is how does the story of Jesus make sense without the story of the Passover? He is, after all, our Passover Lamb. We are saved from damnation and death by his blood.

So what gives? Why do we not consider the Passover as core to our story as we do the cross? To this day, Passover is the central celebration of the Jewish people. But it is a bit of a novelty for most Christians. Many have observed it a time or two, but it's not a signal event in our year. I am asking: Why not? Because this is Jesus' story, it is our story.

Today's text makes it explicitly clear. God expects his people to remember and celebrate the Passover.

"Commemorate this day, the day you came out of Egypt, out of the land of slavery, because the Lord brought you out of it with a mighty hand."

I think the reason we don't do this is because we don't think of them (the Israelites) as us. Permit me to be emphatic. We are them. Those ancient Israelites are us. This is our story as much as it was their story. It doesn't matter that most of us are Gentiles.

Perhaps the most unfortunate words in all the Bible, and I am not even sure they are considered part of the inspired text, are "Old Testament" and "New Testament." The Bible, from Genesis to Revelation, is one story, and it is our story— the story of Father, Son, and Holy Spirit. The New Testament is not the story of Jesus. The whole Bible is the story of Jesus.

It brings me back to my favorite verse from today's text:

"On that day tell your son, 'I do this because of what the Lord did for me when I came out of Egypt.'"

Year after year, as they gathered for the Passover meal, Joseph would tell his young son, Jesus, "I do this because of what the Lord did for me when I came out of Egypt." Hang on. Joseph didn't come out of Egypt. Oh, yes he did. And I did too—even me. Even you. This is more than remembering a story from history. It is commemoration. To commemorate something is to remember it in a way that narrates you into the story itself.

"This observance will be for you like a sign on your hand and a reminder on your forehead that this law of the Lord is to be on your lips. For the Lord brought you out of Egypt with his

mighty hand. You must keep this ordinance at the appointed time year after year."

The Prayer

Father, I want to be a person who says such things. I want to be so immersed in the whole story of you that I never come out. I want to think in its terms, dream in its metaphors, see with its vision, revel in its glory, which is your glory. I confess, I remain ignorant of so much of it. Grant me the joy to bear the fruit of repentance. For you brought me up out of Egypt, even me. Come, Holy Spirit, and train me to be such a person of faith. I pray in Jesus' name, amen.

The Questions

- Are you a student of the whole Bible or have you tended to focus on the New Testament? Why do you think that is?

. . . Follow the Cloud by Day, Fire by Night

53

EXODUS 13:19–22 | Moses took the bones of Joseph with him because Joseph had made the Israelites swear an oath. He had said, "God will surely come to your aid, and then you must carry my bones up with you from this place."

After leaving Sukkoth they camped at Etham on the edge of the desert. By day the LORD went ahead of them in a pillar of cloud to guide them on their way and by night in a pillar of fire to give them light, so that they could travel by day or night. Neither the pillar of cloud by day nor the pillar of fire by night left its place in front of the people.

Consider This

Cloud by day. Fire by night.

Overnight the Israelites moved from the complete and total predictability of slavery to the complete and total unpredictability of freedom. They were not following a strategic plan. They had no initiatives, objectives, or goals. They could only follow God. Every single aspect of their predictable lives was gone. What would they do? They would follow God. Where would they go? They would follow God.

By day the LORD went ahead of them in a pillar of cloud to guide them on their way and by night in a pillar of fire to give them light, so that they could travel by day or night.

We all crave the rhythms, routines, and schedules of a predictable life. It is not a bad thing, but it can lead to the slow onset of spiritual sleep. Our spirits were made for the movement of faith. We were made to hear and be responsive to the voice of God. Something in us wants to domesticate our faith and turn it into a predictable set of routines, to keep it in a comfortable comfort zone, something that enhances our lives but doesn't actually control us. It can be a long way from . . .

Cloud by day. Fire by night.

I know I'm stepping on toes here. So what gives? How do we live in an everyday world and follow a pillar of cloud by day and a pillar of fire by night? First, it's not easy. Second, it takes life-support dependence on Word and Spirit. Third, it requires others in close fellowship. Fourth, it means loosening your grip on yourself and your agenda and your aspirations and dreams. Fifth, it means abandoning yourself to Jesus Christ. Sixth, it means struggling mightily at times (i.e., see Jacob). Seventh it takes years. Eighth, it means the fulfillment of all your deepest hopes and longings, only differently than you ever imagined. Ninth, once you get on this road you won't turn back and you wouldn't trade it for anything the world has to offer.

Cloud by day. Fire by night.

Jesus showed us what it looks like. "Very truly I tell you, the Son can do nothing by himself; he can do only what he sees his Father doing, because whatever the Father does the Son also does" (John 5:19).

We are talking about the abiding life. Less, "Help me, Jesus!" and more, "Have me, Jesus!" We are talking about the narrow way that few find. My hero and mentor, Maxie Dunnam, says it this way, "Most people prefer the hell of a predictable situation rather than risk the joy of an unpredictable one," and then he says it again.

Cloud by day. Fire by night.

The Prayer

Father, I want to be a person who says such things. I confess I am comfortable with my fairly predictable life. Now that all of that is out of the window, I find myself much more open to the joyful unpredictability of following you—cloud by day and fire by night. Release me from my insatiable need to control everything. Come, Holy Spirit, and train me to be such a person of faith. I pray in Jesus' name, amen.

The Question

- Cloud by day. Fire by night. How does that strike you today? It's one thing to follow clear directions; quite another to follow someone who clearly knows where they are going.

54 . . . Trust God When the Way Seems Longer

EXODUS 13:17–18 | When Pharaoh let the people go, God did not lead them on the road through the Philistine country, though that was shorter. For God said, "If they face war, they might change their minds and return to Egypt." So God led the people around by the desert road toward the Red Sea. The Israelites went up out of Egypt ready for battle.

Consider This

We've all heard the cliché bandied about that God doesn't give us anything he knows we can't handle. I've never given it much credence and pretty much filed it in the folder that holds other so-called biblical sayings that aren't in the Bible—like, "God helps those who help themselves." I've never actually seen this phrase in the Bible about God not giving us more than we can handle—until today.

When Pharaoh let the people go, God did not lead them on the road through the Philistine country, though that was shorter. For God said, "If they face war, they might change their minds and return to Egypt."

I bet they were furious. After all they had been through with the bricks-without-straw program and the ten plagues and the bloody lambs and the sudden departure—at night— with all the kids and the sheep and cows and everything else, why on earth would they take the long way around the bend at a time like this? Can you imagine the arm-chair quarter-backing cycling through the ranks? Did Moses just not know the shortcut? Did he think they couldn't defeat the Philistines? After all, the text tells us they left Egypt "ready for battle." To the average Israelite, the whole thing must have felt very questionable. Truth be told, the plan would soon go from questionable to certifiably insane.

God knew. He knew what they could handle and what they could not handle. God knew the mileage differential between the two routes. He knew the soldier count in the Philistine armies and he knew what the Israelite body count would be on the other side of a battle. He knew they would be ready to turn around and go back to Egypt, settle back into their slavish existence, and count it all as a bad dream. God chose not to give them more than he knew they could handle.

Instead, he would take them by a longer route in a way that felt like lost wandering only to arrive at a dead end and their impending doom. God knew they could handle this; perhaps because it would put them in the kind of impossible situation from which only God could save them. Isn't that how it goes?

We can trust God. He engineers our circumstances beyond our knowing. Often it will not make sense to us at the time. At times, it will seem like the worst possible thing has happened; that we have gone from bad to worse, from lost to hopeless. Our prayers seem to bounce off the ceiling. God has a higher plan; a better plan, with endless contingencies, and everything can ultimately be worked together for our good and God's glory. Keep on trusting. Cloud by day. Fire by night. Never give up. Death on Friday. Resurrection on Sunday.

So God led the people around by the desert road toward the Red Sea.

Though I feel lost and in the valley of the shadow of death, yet I will trust him.

The Prayer

Father, I want to be a person who says such things. I confess I wonder at your ways and I second-guess your plans. The better way seems so clear to me, yet I know your ways are higher and better than mine. You see the end from the beginning. You see the things that are not as though they were. I am so tempted by the shorter route and the easier way. Teach me to trust the long road and to know you will not give me more than I can bear. Come, Holy Spirit, and train me to be such a person of faith. I pray in Jesus' name, amen.

The Questions

- Have you witnessed or experienced a situation that didn't make sense at all but that later worked itself into unforeseeable redemptive outcomes? Are you in such a situation now that has yet to resolve into any form of redemption?

. . . Make Camp in the Middle of Chaos

55

EXODUS 14:1–4 | Then the LORD said to Moses, "Tell the Israelites to turn back and encamp near Pi Hahiroth, between Migdol and the sea. They are to encamp by the sea, directly opposite Baal Zephon. Pharaoh will think, 'The Israelites are wandering around the land in confusion, hemmed in by the desert.' And I will harden Pharaoh's heart, and he will pursue them. But I will gain glory for myself through Pharaoh and all his army, and the Egyptians will know that I am the LORD." So the Israelites did this.

Consider This

I'm going to coin a saying as we begin today: We need the mind of Christ to think the thoughts of God. Try saying that with a bit of iambic pentameter (heartbeat rhythm). We need-the mind-of Christ-to think-the thoughts-of God.

Why? Because the thoughts of God are confounding to the minds of people. Look at today's text. God wanted Pharaoh to pursue his people. Why would God want this? So he could defeat Pharaoh and his army. God's strategy? Make it appear to Pharaoh that the Israelites were lost and confused. You know what that felt like for the Israelites? They felt lost and confused. It felt like they were doomed. Meanwhile, Pharaoh could taste the victory. It was literally a worst-case scenario for the Israelites. Everything must have seemed so wrong to them at the time. Why would God put them through so much and bring them so far, only to let them perish like this? Short answer: he wouldn't.

Maybe you've heard the saying, "Not all who wander are lost." Israel proved the point. You may be in the midst of the lowest moment of your life. You may feel lost and confused and in despair. It may even feel like it's all your fault. Renounce despair and look to God. He has a plan.

Remember, the thoughts of God are confounding to the minds of people. How do we know this? First witness—Isaiah:

> "For my thoughts are not your thoughts,
>> neither are your ways my ways,"
>>> declares the LORD.
> "As the heavens are higher than the earth,
>> so are my ways higher than your ways
>> and my thoughts than your thoughts." (Isa. 55:8–9)

Second witness—Paul: "For the foolishness of God is wiser than human wisdom, and the weakness of God is stronger than human strength" (1 Cor. 1:25).

So back to our text of the day. Did you pick up on the confounding absurdity of the instructions?

"Tell the Israelites to turn back and encamp near Pi Hahiroth, between Migdol and the sea."

Translation: "Not only does it appear you are lost and doomed to certain destruction, I want you to make camp there."

In the life of following Jesus in pursuit of the will of God it can feel like a holy-ground burning-bush encounter last week and a holy-hell house fire the next. Don't forget—God has a plan. God can work his best magic in our worst messes. It takes growing up in our faith to grasp this. It's why we must "have the mind of Christ" (1 Cor. 2:16).

We need the mind of Christ to think the thoughts of God. What is the mind of Christ? The mind of Christ is a cultivated faith that trusts God with all one's heart and leans not on our own understanding (see Proverbs 3:5)—even in the most desperate situations; no, especially in the most desperate situations. To gain the mind of Christ we must fix our eyes on Jesus: "For the message of the cross is foolishness to those who are perishing, but to us who are being saved it is the power of God" (1 Cor. 1:18).

It can feel like making camp in the middle of chaos.

The Prayer

Father, I want to be a person who says such things. I confess that your thoughts and ways are higher than my thoughts and ways. I also believe you can give me the mind of Christ. Open my eyes to really see Jesus, in your Word and in the world. I want to think thoughts after you, Lord. I want your ways to become my ways. Come, Holy Spirit, and train me to be such a person of faith. I pray in Jesus' name, amen.

The Questions

- Have you experienced or witnessed one of these situations where the thoughts and ways of God were confounding to conventional wisdom? Are you in one of those situations now?

56 . . . Become Students of Divine Deliverance

EXODUS 14:5–9 | When the king of Egypt was told that the people had fled, Pharaoh and his officials changed their minds about them and said, "What have we done? We have let the Israelites go and have lost their services!" So he had his chariot made ready and took his army with him. He took six hundred of the best chariots, along with all the other chariots of Egypt, with officers over all of them. The Lord hardened the heart of Pharaoh king of Egypt, so that he pursued the Israelites, who were marching out boldly. The Egyptians—all Pharaoh's horses and chariots, horsemen and troops—pursued the Israelites and overtook them as they camped by the sea near Pi Hahiroth, opposite Baal Zephon.

Consider This

Pharaoh had one priority: building his kingdom. The God of Israel also had one priority: building his kingdom. Pharaoh was looking for slaves; God wanted sons and daughters. This is the perennial battle. Every soul hangs in the balance: slave or son/daughter. Will we succumb to the slavery of building the kingdoms of this world, or will we become sons and daughters and inherit the now-and-still-coming kingdom of God?

Pharaoh represents to us the powers of darkness, and darkness will not release its slaves without a fierce battle. The text is careful to tell us Pharaoh sent six hundred of the best chariots along with all the other chariots of Egypt. He sent the entire army with many officers, troops, horses, and riders. Finally, Pharaoh rode into battle himself in his own chariot. This is an extraordinary response and extremely lethal. This is the power of darkness.

There is a larger principle at work here. It is the principal of the principalities of darkness: the kingdom and principalities of darkness will not readily or willingly or easily release their prisoners. Human effort is of no avail. It requires the delivering power of God Almighty. The power of darkness is extremely powerful; far more powerful than mere mortals. Compared to the power of God, the power of darkness is no power at all.

Divine deliverance is a complex process and it can take a protracted period of time. The main reason for this is the preference of God to deploy human agents in the process of divine deliverance. Look at the long-game strategy of deliverance in this instance. It began in the midst of a period of intense darkness in Egypt—the lawful murder of all the Israelite baby boys in the country. God began with a pair of courageous parents who made a way for their baby boy to escape death. God used the household of Pharaoh to save this child who would grow up to become Pharaoh's nemesis. This son would grow up witnessing the cruelty of Pharaoh as an oppressor of God's people. Moses grew up with the power paradigm of Pharaoh, leading him to commit murder to defeat a murderer. Moses needed deliverance. At age forty God took Moses out of Egypt, and over the next forty years he took Egypt out of Moses. Are you watching the time line here? It took eighty years for this plan to come to launch.

After launch and the unforeseen bricks-without-straw program, Moses had a near mutiny on his hands. It took many meetings with repeated requests and ten catastrophic plagues to bring Pharaoh to his knees. This whole matter of divine deliverance was extremely complex, profoundly chaotic, and maddeningly unpredictable at every juncture. Despite all of this, God was in complete control, every step of the way.

As we observed yesterday, God delivered the Israelites from Egypt in one night. The deliverance was hardly over. Though Pharaoh was brought to his knees, he quickly got back up. It must have seemed to everyone on the field he would have things back in hand overnight. God had other plans.

I labor to make this point for two reasons. First, we need to read far more deeply into these ancient stories of our faith because they hold deep wisdom and insight. They hold much deeper faith for the sake of the second reason: we also need to understand the sophisticated complexities of the kingdom of darkness in our own time in our own lives, families, and communities, our utter inability and incompetence to combat it on our own with our own resources and the incredible, unstoppable power of God over darkness for us who believe. We are living in an age where we desperately need divine deliverance from the deep, deep infestation of compounded darkness in every aspect of the world around us. It will take a great awakening. Hence, we sow.

It strikes me to invite the apostle Paul to say our closing prayer today.

The Prayer

I pray that the eyes of your heart may be enlightened in order that you may know the hope to which he has called you, the riches of his glorious inheritance in his holy people, and his incomparably great power for us who believe. That power is the same as the mighty strength he exerted when he raised Christ from the dead and seated him at his right hand in the heavenly realms, far above all rule and authority, power and dominion, and every name that is invoked, not only in the present age but also in the one to come. (Eph. 1:18–21)

In Jesus' name, amen.

The Question
- On a scale of 1 to 10, with 10 being the highest, where do you rate your knowledge, understanding, and experience of the ministry of divine deliverance?

57 . . . Know 1 Percent Is Enough

EXODUS 14:10–14 | As Pharaoh approached, the Israelites looked up, and there were the Egyptians, marching after them. They were terrified and cried out to the LORD. They said to Moses, "Was it because there were no graves in Egypt that you brought us to the desert to die? What have you done to us by bringing us out of Egypt? Didn't we say to you in Egypt, 'Leave us alone; let us serve the Egyptians'? It would have been better for us to serve the Egyptians than to die in the desert!"

Moses answered the people, "Do not be afraid. Stand firm and you will see the deliverance the LORD will bring you today. The Egyptians you see today you will never see again. The LORD will fight for you; you need only to be still."

Consider This

Today's text unfolds the worst-case possible, doomsday scenario. The newly freed Israelite former slaves stared down the barrel of the most powerful army in the world. Red Sea on one side; Pharaoh's army on the other. These are the moments that expose our deepest dispositions. Will we find fear or faith? Two people can face the very same reality and have diabolically opposite responses. We see it here on full display.

The Israelites asked three questions and made a declaration. Moses offered three responses and made a proclamation. Note how they intertwine and correspond as follows:

Question #1: Was it because there were no graves in
   Egypt that you brought us to the desert to die?
Response #1: Do not be afraid.

Question #2: What have you done to us by bringing us
   out of Egypt?
Response #2: Stand firm and you will see the deliverance the Lord will bring you today.

Question #3: Didn't we say to you in Egypt, "Leave us
   alone; let us serve the Egyptians"?
Response #3: The Egyptians you see today you will
   never see again.

Declaration of fear: It would have been better for us to
   serve the Egyptians than to die in the desert!
Declaration of faith: The Lord will fight for you; you
   need only to be still.

Fear is a given. The question is faith. Here's the interesting
calculus of faith. Think of a spectrum of 0 to 100-percent.
What part of the spectrum will be taken up by fear? In this
case, the Israelites were at 100-percent fear on the spectrum. There was no room for faith in their response. Moses,
however, spoke to them of the power of God. Moses knew
all he needed was a movement of 1 percent to win the day.
If he could push their fear back from 100 to 99 percent, it
would leave room for a 1-percent faith response. Moses knew
1 percent was all he needed. So did Jesus: "Truly I tell you,
if you have faith as small as a mustard seed, you can say to

this mountain, 'Move from here to there,' and it will move. Nothing will be impossible for you" (Matt. 17:20).

The issue is not the size of one's faith, but the strength of their God. It's why when we want to see faith rise up we don't try to talk people into having more faith. Nor are we likely to be successful in trying to talk them out of their fear. We win when we witness to them about the nature, character, and power of God. One percent is all it takes. In another sense, Moses was the 1 percent:

Moses answered the people, "Do not be afraid. Stand firm and you will see the deliverance the Lord will bring you today. The Egyptians you see today you will never see again. The Lord will fight for you; you need only to be still."

The Prayer

Father, I want to be a person who says such things. I confess how I can put the emphasis on my faith or lack thereof and miss the point of who my faith is in. I don't want to have faith in faith, but in almighty God. Help me grow true, real, rich, and deep faith—even a mustard seed–sized faith. I would rather have 1 percent of the real thing than 99 percent of anything else. Come, Holy Spirit, and train me to be such a person of faith. I pray in Jesus' name, amen.

The Questions

- Do you tend to be a person who thinks they don't have enough faith? How does this 1-percent principle impact you? Am I making sense here?

. . . Share in the Glory of God

58

EXODUS 14:15–18 | Then the Lord said to Moses, "Why are you crying out to me? Tell the Israelites to move on. Raise your staff and stretch out your hand over the sea to divide the water so that the Israelites can go through the sea on dry ground. I will harden the hearts of the Egyptians so that they will go in after them. And I will gain glory through Pharaoh and all his army, through his chariots and his horsemen. The Egyptians will know that I am the Lord when I gain glory through Pharaoh, his chariots and his horsemen."

Consider This

I absolutely love this moment. Moses had just given his best *Braveheart* speech: "Do not be afraid. Stand firm and you will see the deliverance the Lord will bring you today. The Egyptians you see today you will never see again. The Lord will fight for you; you need only to be still" (14:13–14).

Then, in an apparent contradiction of Moses' uber cine-matically spiritual message to the Israelites, God says this:

"Why are you crying out to me? Tell the Israelites to move on."

Based on what he said, it appears Moses expected God was going to hurl bolts of lightning and destroy the Egyptian army. He expected God would slay the Egyptians as the Israelites stood by and watched. Clearly, the notion of parting the waters of the sea would not have crossed even their wildest imaginings. There was no category for such a thing. Even more surprising than this is how it would happen.

Raise your staff and stretch out your hand over the sea to divide the water so that the Israelites can go through the sea on dry ground.

God called Moses to part the sea. God would give the power, but he wanted Moses to do it: "Raise your staff and stretch out your hand." This is truly extraordinary. Moses was not an interested bystander or onlooker; he was an agent of the deliverance of God. Second only to the resurrection of Jesus Christ, the deliverance of the Israelites through the Red Sea is the single most incredible mighty act of God in human history.

So why didn't God just do it himself? Why Moses and his staff and his outstretched hand? I have a theory: God wanted to share his glory with Moses. I know many will not be comfortable with this idea, but let me make the case. Throughout Scripture, we see three primary dimensions of the grace of God. We see saving grace; most often referred to as justifying grace or the gift of the salvation of God. We see purifying grace; most often referred to as sanctifying grace or the gift of the holiness of God. We see radiant grace; most often referred to as glorifying grace or the gift of the glory of God.

If God wants to gift us with justifying grace and sanctifying grace, why would he not want to gift us with glorifying grace? He would. The problem is not with God but with us. We do not have a category for such a thing, unless we consider it something reserved for a Christian's death. These graces and gifts are sequential and progressive in nature. We should not expect to see glorifying grace among the young and less mature believers. We should expect to see it in the older and more mature believers (in the period of life I call one's "kingdom prime.") Moses was eighty years old, after all.

Hear me clearly. Glorifying grace does not mean we get the glory. The glory is God's. He empowers us to share and participate in his glory; to do glorious things in the earth by the power of his holy love. The problem most of us have in accepting such teaching is we think glory is a zero-sum game. There is only so much glory and to the extent that I get any glory it robs God of his glory. This is a misconception. We don't *get* glory, rather we are given the gift of participating and sharing in God's glory. It is of infinite quantity and quality. Just like the gift of holiness requires the prerequisite gift of redemption, so the gift of glory requires the prerequisite gift of holiness. And all of this is the gift of God in Christ Jesus, plain to see in Scripture.

With Moses, we get an extraordinary precursor glimpse of glorifying grace; of a human being participating in the glory of God. I am not for one second even slightly inclined to give the glory to Moses. I just want to revel in it all and maybe hold the staff for a minute! In Jesus, we see what God intends it to look like when a human being participates fully in the glorifying grace of God. It is the gift of God for those who are willing to believe that union with God is not only possible, but the plan. Jesus said, "Very truly I tell you, whoever believes in me will do the works I have been doing, and they will do even greater things than these, because I am going to the Father" (John 14:12).

Now hear this in Jesus' High Priestly prayer in John 17: "I have given them the glory that you gave me, that they may be one as we are one—I in them and you in me—so that they may be brought to complete unity. Then the world will know that you sent me and have loved them even as you have loved me" (vv. 22–23).

I know. These are big ideas over coffee on a Saturday morning. They are God-sized ideas.

"Raise your staff and stretch out your hand over the sea to divide the water so that the Israelites can go through the sea on dry ground."

The Prayer

Father, I want to be a person who says such things. Thank you for the gift of saving grace. Because of this I am redeemed. Thank you for the gift of sanctifying grace. Because of this I am being made holy like you are holy. And thank you for the gift of glorifying grace. I struggle with this one and yet I welcome it. Lead me into the country of deep union with you and your people such that I can revel in participating in your glory—on earth as it is in heaven. I will dare to believe. Come, Holy Spirit, and train me to be such a person of faith. I pray in Jesus' name, amen.

The Questions

- Do you struggle with this teaching about glorifying grace? Why? Do you aspire to it? Will you stretch to believe it?

. . . Cultivate Holy Imagination

59

EXODUS 14:19–20 | Then the angel of God, who had been traveling in front of Israel's army, withdrew and went behind them. The pillar of cloud also moved from in front and stood behind them, coming between the armies of Egypt and Israel. Throughout the night the cloud brought darkness to the one side and light to the other side; so neither went near the other all night long.

Consider This

Maybe you've heard the story of the seven-year-old boy who learned the story of the Israelites and the Red Sea in Sunday school. Upon being asked by his mother what he learned in class, he said:

> "Well, Mom, our teacher told us how God sent Moses behind enemy lines on a rescue mission to lead the Israelite people out of Egypt. When he got to the Red Sea, he had his army build a pontoon bridge and all the people walked across safely. Then, he radioed

headquarters for reinforcements. They scrambled a squadron of F-16 Falcon Fighter Jets to blow up the bridge and all the Israelites were saved."

"Now, Billy, is that really what your teacher taught you?" his mother asked.

"Well, no, Mom, but if I told you what the teacher said, you'd never believe it in a million years!"

Today's text gives us the incredible true story of what happened on that night at the Red Sea. Here it is again. It merits a second reading to take it all in:

Then the angel of God, who had been traveling in front of Israel's army, withdrew and went behind them. The pillar of cloud also moved from in front and stood behind them, coming between the armies of Egypt and Israel. Throughout the night the cloud brought darkness to the one side and light to the other side; so neither went near the other all night long.

Imagine trying to explain your iPhone or the Internet to your great-great-grandmother. Where would you start? You would say things like, "Grandma, I can talk to a person in London, England, right now while seeing their face on the screen and sending them a photograph of my children via a text message at the same time." What is she going to do with that? Would she even remotely believe it, even if we demonstrated it before her very eyes? All we could do was give her the outlandish, incredible, unbelievable, yet true, facts. That is all Moses did here. He gave us the outlandish, incredible, unbelievable, yet true, facts. It is one thing to try to explain something from today to an earlier time. Moses was telling the story of something way back then to people thousands of years hence—believe it or not.

Angels and armies, pillars of cloud and fire, as a group of millions of refugees walked toward an impenetrable wall of water (a.k.a. the Red Sea) while being pursued by the most formidable army on earth. And then we get this:

> Then Moses stretched out his hand over the sea, and all that night the Lord drove the sea back with a strong east wind and turned it into dry land. The waters were divided, and the Israelites went through the sea on dry ground, with a wall of water on their right and on their left. (vv. 21–22)

Rather than say anything else here, I want to invite you to an exercise of holy imagination. I want you to behold this ancient scene. First, read the text Exodus 14:19–22 out loud. Your ears need to hear it. When we read, the information enters through our eyes and goes straight to our brain. Remember, we walk by faith, not by sight (see 2 Corinthians 5:7). Faith does not come through sight, but by hearing. Faith, through hearing (see Romans 10:17), gives something beyond mere eyesight. Faith gives our heart and soul the vision of God. It's why Paul prays in Ephesians 1:17 for God to open the eyes of our hearts. After hearing the text read aloud, I want you to ask the Holy Spirit to open the eyes of your heart to behold this vision—and open your heart to visualize it happening, in as much detail as your Spirit-empowered imagination can muster.

Then Moses stretched out his hand over the sea, and all that night the LORD drove the sea back with a strong east wind and turned it into dry land.

The Prayer

> I keep asking that the God of our Lord Jesus Christ, the glorious Father, may give you the Spirit of wisdom and revelation, so that you may know him better. I pray that the eyes of your heart may be enlightened in order that you may know the hope to which he has called you, the riches of his glorious inheritance in his holy people, and his incomparably great power for us who believe. That power is the same as the mighty strength he exerted when he raised Christ from the dead and seated him at his right hand in the heavenly realms, far above all rule and authority, power and dominion, and every name that is invoked, not only in the present age but also in the one to come. (Eph. 1:17–21)

Come, Holy Spirit, and train me to be such a person of faith. I pray in Jesus' name, amen.

The Questions

- Did you do it—the exercise of holy imagination? What did you see?

. . . Crave Clarity in Chaos

60

EXODUS 14:23–25 | The Egyptians pursued them, and all Pharaoh's horses and chariots and horsemen followed them into the sea. During the last watch of the night the LORD looked down from the pillar of fire and cloud at the Egyptian army and threw it into confusion. He jammed the wheels of their chariots so that they had difficulty driving. And the Egyptians said, "Let's get away from the Israelites! The LORD is fighting for them against Egypt."

Consider This

As you might imagine, I get a fair amount of reader mail. Most of it is encouragement, for which I am grateful. Sometimes a reader takes issue with something I have written, which I appreciate and try to respond to. Often, I get questions like this one: Why did the Egyptian army enter the water trap when its occurrence obviously defied all laws of physics?

Here is my initial response: bloodlust, greed, and the maintenance of their own kingdom and way of life. The slaves were their Dow Jones Industrial average.

It's a good question. In the best of times, people make irrational decisions. In the midst of unrelenting chaos, people make horribly irrational decisions. The Israelites walked into the sea pursuing the kingdom of God. Pharaoh and his armies charged into the sea chasing the kingdom of Egypt. They pursued the protection of their way of life.

Life really comes down to such a simple choice. Sometimes it takes a plague, or ten, to bring it to such clarity. The rest of the time it can be so many shiny things whirring around our heads and filling up our phones. For so many, it's coffee in the morning and wine at night and a long day's labor between to get to the next income bracket with better schools, nicer vacations, and richer retirement accounts. We live from deer season to turkey season, from the Super Bowl to the World Series, from Augusta National to the Final Four. And, to be clear, none of these things are bad at all. They are good, yet they can keep us in such a state of constant distraction and preoccupation we miss the real point and purpose of our one life. Coffee and beer; lunch and supper; Saturday and Sunday—and where on earth is God in all of that?

Thoreau put it this way: "Most people lead lives of quiet desperation, and they go to the grave with the song still in them." Blaise Pascal said it thus: "We run heedlessly into the abyss after putting something in front of us to stop us from seeing it." Most don't realize it until they are miles into the Red Sea, chasing after a mirage, surrounded by water walls threatening to become water falls.

Jesus said it so decisively and clearly: "But seek first his kingdom and his righteousness, and all these things will be given to you as well" (Matt. 6:33). For so many churchgoing (or at least church-saluting) Christians, it can be more like,

"Seek all these things, ask for God's help to get them, and consider yourself blessed by God when they come. And the kingdom of God and his righteousness will be added unto you." It is the peak of deception. God and the things of God occupy such a small compartment in far too many lives. Church fills such a stale, stifling, and predictable category. When will we finally wake up? The thing we must come to crave in these days of chaos is the gift of clarity. This is a moment for deep-soul clarity.

It brings me no pleasure to say things like this, and yet it gives me the hope of joy that some will wake up and look up and light up to the life they were made for. It won't mean giving up everything you enjoy—not for a minute. It will mean something infinitely greater to live for. That is awakening. And it's never too late. Jesus—not stale religion, not a caricature of church, not self-righteous pompous asses; just Jesus—he's better than the best.

The Prayer

Father, I want to be a person who says such things. I want you to forgive me for being the kind of person at times who makes people want to run away from Jesus. I confess I can be more concerned about the stock market than the souls of my friends and neighbors. I pray for awakening in myself to come alive to ultimate things, to more of you, to what life is really for and about. Come, Holy Spirit, and train me to be such a person of faith. I pray in Jesus' name, amen.

The Questions

- If I've offended you today, will you forgive me? And will you ask yourself why you were offended?

61 . . . Understand the Wrath of God

EXODUS 14:26–28 | Then the Lᴏʀᴅ said to Moses, "Stretch out your hand over the sea so that the waters may flow back over the Egyptians and their chariots and horsemen." Moses stretched out his hand over the sea, and at daybreak the sea went back to its place. The Egyptians were fleeing toward it, and the Lᴏʀᴅ swept them into the sea. The water flowed back and covered the chariots and horsemen—the entire army of Pharaoh that had followed the Israelites into the sea. Not one of them survived.

Consider This

There is so much to deal with in all of these texts with Moses, Pharaoh, the Israelites, the Egyptians, the sea, and the wind. It is so easy to get lost in the details—to become preoccupied with the faith of Moses, the fear of the Israelites, the hard-heartedness of Pharaoh, and so on. We can draw lessons about fear, faith, obedience, and rebellion until the cows come home. We can walk around the burning bush a thousand times, get a different life application each time, and still miss the whole point of the whole thing.

There is only one thing with which we must deal. This is not a story about Moses or Pharaoh or the Israelites or the Egyptians. It's not a story about Abraham, Isaac, Jacob, or Joseph. It is not a story about you or me. This is the story of God.

This story and these stories are meant to do one thing and one thing alone: to reveal the God of heaven and earth. I am convicted at just how easy it can be to deal with everything else in the text but God. It can all be so interesting and helpful and meaningful and yet stultifyingly trifling. Isn't that a great word by the way—*stultifyingly*!

In today's text we are drawn to the awe-inspiring sovereignty of almighty God. We see both the unity and integrity of God's character in two very different expressions and outcomes that are really only one thing. We see the love of God on full display, delivering the Israelites through the Red Sea. And at the same time, we see the wrath of God, bringing the Egyptians to utter ruin and desolation. For my money, the most powerful words in today's text are these: *the LORD swept them into the sea*. The same waters through which Israel was delivered proved to be the death of the Egyptians. The same God brings deliverance and doom through the same act at the same time. The love of God is the wrath of God. They cannot be separated or divided, as they are seamless dimensions of the same whole.

Allow me to correct a common misconception at this point. People don't like to deal with the idea of the wrath of God. This is largely because they associate the concept of wrath with some angry man in their past. The wrath of God must not be equated with the anger of God as though wrath were some kind of divine emotional response. The wrath of God is simply the effect of his nature on all who are unprepared for his unmitigated presence. The wrath of God is what happens when the holy love of God encounters sin. They simply cannot coexist.

Consider the image of fire. Fire either burns or refines; it destroys or purifies. The outcome depends not on the nature of the fire but on the properties of the substance entering the flames. Straw will fare quite differently than steel. Interestingly, the writer of Hebrews reminds us: "for our 'God is a consuming fire'" (Heb. 12:29). It's why earlier the same writer warns: "It is a dreadful thing to fall into the hands of the living God" (Heb. 10:31).

The wrath of God is the effect of the holy love of God on sin.

It is why the Gospels all begin with John the Baptist preaching a baptism of repentance from sin, with the stark warning: "You brood of vipers! Who warned you to flee from the coming wrath?" (Luke 3:7).

Paul makes this profoundly clear in his letter to the Roman Christians: "The wrath of God is being revealed from heaven against all the godlessness and wickedness of people, who suppress the truth by their wickedness" (Rom. 1:18).

Paul goes on to make clear: "for all have sinned and fall short of the glory of God" (Rom. 3:23).

And this sets the stage for the merciful miracle of the gospel of Jesus Christ, as Paul proclaims: "But God demonstrates his own love for us in this: While we were still sinners, Christ died for us. Since we have now been justified by his blood, how much more shall we be saved from God's wrath through him!" (Rom. 5:8–9).

And to the Corinthians, he says it even more clearly:

> We are therefore Christ's ambassadors, as though God were making his appeal through us. We implore you on Christ's behalf: Be reconciled to God. God made him who had no sin to be sin for us, so that in him we might become the righteousness of God. (2 Cor. 5:20–21)

At the cross we simultaneously behold the great mystery of Christ—the wrath of God against sin and the love of God for sinners—and we are saved.

From the parting of the sea to a hill far away, our God reigns and his love endures forever.

The Prayer

Father, I want to be a person who says such things. I want to see you, high and lifted up, holy and exalted, a consuming fire and yet a merciful Father. I want to behold you. Open the eyes of my heart that I might see you. Lord Jesus Christ, Son of God, have mercy on me, a sinner. Lord Jesus Christ, Son of

God, have mercy on me, a son/a daughter. Lord Jesus Christ, Son of God, have mercy on me, a saint. Come, Holy Spirit, and train me to be such a person of faith. I pray in Jesus' name, amen.

The Questions

- What are your reflections on the wrath of God and the love of God being two dimensions of the same reality? Do you struggle with the wrath of God? Why or why not?

62 . . . Can Walk Right Through

EXODUS 14:29–31 | But the Israelites went through the sea on dry ground, with a wall of water on their right and on their left. That day the Lord saved Israel from the hands of the Egyptians, and Israel saw the Egyptians lying dead on the shore. And when the Israelites saw the mighty hand of the Lord displayed against the Egyptians, the people feared the Lord and put their trust in him and in Moses his servant.

Consider This

This must be one of the most astonishing sentences in all of the Bible:

But the Israelites went through the sea on dry ground, with a wall of water on their right and on their left.

The New International Version chose the word "went," but the Hebrew word is *halak* and it means "walked."

They walked through the sea.

It is one thing to walk on water, but quite another to walk through the sea.

They walked through the sea, Scripture is careful to tell us, "on dry ground." Not wet or muddy ground, but dry ground.

More than a million people walked through the sea on dry ground.

God did this for his people. He did this for us:

> While they were eating, Jesus took bread, and when he had given thanks, he broke it and gave it to his disciples, saying, "Take and eat; this is my body."
>
> Then he took a cup, and when he had given thanks, he gave it to them, saying, "Drink from it, all of you. This is my blood of the covenant, which is poured out for many for the forgiveness of sins. I tell you, I will not drink from this fruit of the vine from now on until that day when I drink it new with you in my Father's kingdom." (Matt. 26:26–29)

God did this for his people. He did this for us.

When we gather at this first table we remember that Last Supper, and when we remember that Last Supper, we remember the Passover and the Red Sea. As a consequence of this, billions of us have walked through the sea on dry ground.

Just like we were there when they crucified our Lord, we were there when God parted the waters of the Red Sea.

"Sometimes it causes me to tremble."

The Prayer

Father, I want to be a person who says such things. You are truly a marvel. I stand amazed at this mighty act of redemption and judgment you rendered at the Red Sea. Even more, I stand in awe of the mighty act of redemption and judgment you performed at the cross. This is truly amazing love. Give me the grace to truly perceive it, more than before, to grasp and be grasped by it. Take me there and I shall never be the same. Come, Holy Spirit, and train me to be such a person of faith. I pray in Jesus' name, amen.

The Question

- How will it be different this time around?

63 ... Know Their Context

LUKE 23:44–49 | It was now about noon, and darkness came over the whole land until three in the afternoon, for the sun stopped shining. And the curtain of the temple was torn in two. Jesus called out with a loud voice, "Father, into your hands I commit my spirit." When he had said this, he breathed his last.

The centurion, seeing what had happened, praised God and said, "Surely this was a righteous man." When all the people who had gathered to witness this sight saw what took place, they beat their breasts and went away. But all those who knew him, including the women who had followed him from Galilee, stood at a distance, watching these things.

Consider This

There is a word here I never really noticed until today. Perhaps you haven't either. I suspect not. I suspect you may be like me in that I think I know the story of Jesus' passion. After all, I've read it a thousand times. Because of this, I am always tempted to not read it again. I mean, it's spread out across four different books and it feels largely redundant except for the unique parts each holds, and I assume I know those well enough. At least this is how my lazy mind works.

Might this verse awaken a part of my preoccupied soul? It brings me to the text I never noticed before.

It wasn't the three hours of darkness at high noon, or the tearing of the temple curtain from top to bottom, or Jesus' cries from the cross, or the Roman centurion's declaration of faith. It was this line:

But all those who knew him, including the women who had followed him from Galilee, stood at a distance, watching these things.

There is a group of people standing off to the side, at a distance. They are watching all of this unfold. We don't know how many there were in the group. We know there were women from Galilee. We know them simply as "all those who knew him." Today, I am watching them watching him, and I find myself being drawn to walk into their sad circle and watch all "these things" with them. We are them—"all those who knew him." We aren't on the front row. We are standing at a distance "watching these things."

I was on a call with my band and as one of my bandmates prayed for me, he prayed I would "know my context." I felt like I had found a diamond on the ground. I have been pulling it out of my pocket all day and looking at its many facets. What is my context?

Many of us find ourselves in a liminal context. It means an in-between place, a threshold of sorts. We are in the middle of something where everything seems to be shifting. Something deep within tells us we are not who we were before this present moment, and yet we don't quite know who we will be on the other side of it. On the one hand, we know ourselves and our propensity to snap back into the same old us. On the other hand, we know Jesus, and find ourselves deeply aware of the possibilities of walking out of this time into a new way of living and being our true selves. This strange context of life in liminality, of standing at a distance—it could be the gifted space we needed most.

The Prayer

Father, I want to be a person who says such things. I want to pray with Jesus today, as he gave up his life that I might be given mine. "Father, into your hands I commit my spirit." Thank you, Jesus, for showing me this way of giving up my life to the Father that I might truly receive my life from him. I have clung to my spirit long enough. It is time to commit it to you, completely, unreservedly, with abandon. Into your hands, Lord Jesus, I commit my spirit. Come, Holy Spirit, and train me to be such a person of faith. I pray in Jesus' name, amen.

The Questions

- Do you find yourself in a liminal context at this time in your life? Or are you tending to drift off to sleep? How might you respond to the work of the Spirit right now? Otherwise, what might waking up look like?

. . . Follow the Women 64

EXODUS 15:1–18 ESV | Then Moses and the people of Israel sang this song to the LORD, saying,

"I will sing to the LORD, for he has triumphed gloriously;
　the horse and his rider he has thrown into the sea.
The LORD is my strength and my song,
　and he has become my salvation;
this is my God, and I will praise him,
　my father's God, and I will exalt him.
The LORD is a man of war;
　the LORD is his name.

"Pharaoh's chariots and his host he cast into the sea,
　and his chosen officers were sunk in the Red Sea.
The floods covered them;

they went down into the depths like a stone.
Your right hand, O LORD, glorious in power,
    your right hand, O LORD, shatters the enemy.
In the greatness of your majesty you overthrow your
    adversaries;
    you send out your fury; it consumes them like stubble.
At the blast of your nostrils the waters piled up;
    the floods stood up in a heap;
    the deeps congealed in the heart of the sea.
The enemy said, 'I will pursue, I will overtake,
    I will divide the spoil, my desire shall have its fill of them.
    I will draw my sword; my hand shall destroy them.'
You blew with your wind; the sea covered them;
    they sank like lead in the mighty waters.

"Who is like you, O LORD, among the gods?
    Who is like you, majestic in holiness,
    awesome in glorious deeds, doing wonders?
You stretched out your right hand;
    the earth swallowed them.

"You have led in your steadfast love the people whom you
    have redeemed;
    you have guided them by your strength to your holy abode.
The peoples have heard; they tremble;
    pangs have seized the inhabitants of Philistia.
Now are the chiefs of Edom dismayed;
    trembling seizes the leaders of Moab;

all the inhabitants of Canaan have melted away.
Terror and dread fall upon them;
  because of the greatness of your arm, they are still as
    a stone,
till your people, O Lord, pass by,
  till the people pass by whom you have purchased.
You will bring them in and plant them on your own
    mountain,
  the place, O Lord, which you have made for your abode,
  the sanctuary, O Lord, which your hands have established.
The Lord will reign forever and ever."

Consider This

I served for eleven years in a very obscure, yet highly coveted post of ministry. I was the dean of the chapel at Asbury Theological Seminary. In the tiny town of Wilmore, in the heart of rural Kentucky, I pastored a thousand or so seminary students (a.k.a. pastors) for eleven gloriously challenging years. In those years, we gathered for worship more than a thousand times. One of those gatherings stands in a category all its own. For many of those years we hosted a gathering known to the history of the worship of the church as "The Easter Vigil."

The Easter Vigil always begins at dark on Holy Saturday. It starts outside of the sanctuary with a fire known as "The New Fire." Once everyone is assembled around this fire, a very tall torch of a candle is lit symbolizing the "Pillar of

Fire" by which God led the Israelites in their deliverance from Egypt. Everyone follows the Pillar of Fire into the sanctuary and the festivities begin. The Easter Vigil is the Super Bowl of worship; a roof-raising journey through twelve readings of Scripture. At the heart of this greatest highlight reel of all time is the parting of the Red Sea followed by the most epic end-zone dance in the history of the world. We know it as Miriam's song and it is today's text:

> Then Miriam the prophetess, the sister of Aaron, took a tambourine in her hand, and all the women went out after her with tambourines and dancing. And Miriam sang to them:

> "Sing to the LORD, for he has triumphed gloriously;
> the horse and his rider he has thrown into the sea."
> (Ex. 15:20–21 ESV)

Let's just say at this point, our Easter Vigil got completely carried away. The birth pangs of resurrection kicked into full gear, leading our labor of liturgical love onward until the stroke of midnight when we shook off the shroud of death and rose up into the resurrection; as though it were happening for the very first time.

Resurrection is Miriam's song times ten to the trillionth power.

Thank God for Miriam and the women of the church, who never lost their nerve. As the twelve scattered to who knows where, the women remained. Last at the cross and the first at the tomb, the women were the apostles to the apostles—the first preachers of the gospel.

"Death is swallowed up in victory."

"O death, where is your victory?

O death, where is your sting?" (1 Cor. 15:54b–55 ESV)

The Prayer

Father, I want to be a person who says such things. Thank you for the women of your kingdom: the Marys and the Marthas and the Miriams. Lord, I want to be in that number when the saints go marching in. Today, I will sing to the Lord, for he has triumphed gloriously; the horse and his rider he has thrown into the sea. Come, Holy Spirit, and train me to be such a person of faith. I pray in Jesus' name, amen.

The Question

- "Sing to the LORD, for he has triumphed gloriously; the horse and his rider he has thrown into the sea." How might this song find its way into your songbook of life right now?

... Proclaim the Risen Christ!

65

LUKE 24:1–12 | On the first day of the week, very early in the morning, the women took the spices they had prepared and went to the tomb. They found the stone rolled away from the tomb, but when they entered, they did not find the body of the Lord Jesus. While they were wondering about this, suddenly two men in clothes that gleamed like lightning stood beside them. In their fright the women bowed down with their faces to the ground, but the men said to them, "Why do you look for the living among the dead? He is not here; he has risen! Remember how he told you, while he was still with you in Galilee: 'The Son of Man must be delivered over to the hands of sinners, be crucified and on the third day be raised again.'" Then they remembered his words.

When they came back from the tomb, they told all these things to the Eleven and to all the others. It was Mary Magdalene, Joanna, Mary the mother of James, and the others with them who told this to the apostles. But they did not believe the women, because their words seemed to them like nonsense. Peter, however, got up and ran to the tomb. Bending over, he saw the strips of linen lying by themselves, and he went away, wondering to himself what had happened.

Consider This

This is my all-time favorite sermon. It happens to be the earliest sermon we have in recorded history outside of the Bible. It was proclaimed by Melito of Sardis, the Bishop of Sardis, who was a prominent leader in the second-century church. He wrote this sermon around the year 167. It is the equivalent of the most spectacular theological fireworks show ever. And now, without further ado, I present to you . . .

On Pascha*

This is the one who comes from heaven onto
the earth for us suffering ones,
and wraps himself in the suffering one
through a virgin womb
and comes as a human.
He accepted the suffering of us suffering ones,
through suffering in a body which could suffer,
and set free the flesh from suffering.
Through the spirit which cannot die
he slew the human-slayer death.
He is the one led like a lamb
and slaughtered like a sheep;
he ransomed us from the worship of the world
as from the land of Egypt,
and he set us free from the slavery of the devil
as from the hand of Pharaoh,
and sealed our souls with his own spirit,
and the members of our body with his blood.
This is the one who clad death in shame
and, as Moses did to Pharaoh,
made the devil grieve.
This is the one who struck down lawlessness

*This excerpt of *On Pascha* by Melito of Sardis (pp. 233–237) was passed on to me by Dr. Lester Ruth, PhD, a liturgical scholar. We used it for several years as part of our celebration of the Easter Vigil at Asbury Theological Seminary during my tenure there as dean of the chapel. A full version of this ancient reading may be found at Melito of Sardis, *On Pascha, with the Fragments of Melito and Other Material Related to Quartodecimas*, translated, introduced, and annotated by Alistair Stewart-Sykes (Crestwood, NY: St. Vladimir's Seminary Press, 2001).

and made injustice childless,
as Moses did in Egypt.
This is the one who delivered us from slavery to freedom,
from darkness into light,
from death into life,
from tyranny into an eternal Kingdom,
and made us a new priesthood,
and a people everlasting for himself.
This is the Pascha of our salvation:
this is the one who in many people endured many things.
This is the one who was murdered in Abel,
tied up in Isaac,
exiled in Jacob,
sold in Joseph,
exposed in Moses,
slaughtered in the lamb,
hunted down in David,
dishonored in the prophets.
This is the one made flesh in a virgin
who was hanged on a tree,
who was buried in the earth,
who was raised from the dead,
who was exalted to the heights of heaven.
This is the lamb slain,
this is the speechless lamb,
this is the one born of Mary the fair ewe,
this is the one taken from the flock,
and led to slaughter.

Who was sacrificed in the evening,
and buried at night;
who was not broken on the tree,
who was not undone in the earth,
who rose from the dead and resurrected humankind from
the grave below.
O mystifying murder! O mystifying injustice!
The master is obscured by his body exposed,
and is not held worthy of a veil to shield him from view.
For this reason the great lights turned away,
and the day was turned to darkness;
to hide the one denuded on the tree,
obscuring not the body of the Lord but human eyes.
For when the people did not tremble, the earth shook.
When the people did not fear, the heavens were afraid.
When the people did not rend their garments, the angel
rent his own.
When the people did not lament, the Lord thundered from
heaven,
and the most high gave voice.
"Who takes issue with me? Let him stand before me.
I set free the condemned.
I gave life to the dead.
I raise up the entombed.
Who will contradict me?"
"It is I," says the Christ,
"I am he who destroys death
and triumphs over the enemy,

and crushes Hades,
and binds the strong man,
and bears humanity off to the heavenly heights."
"It is I," says the Christ,
"So come all families of people,
adulterated with sin,
and receive forgiveness of sins.
For I am your freedom.
I am the Passover of salvation,
I am the Lamb slaughtered for you,
I am your ransom,
I am your life,
I am your light,
I am your salvation,
I am your resurrection,
I am your King.
I shall raise you up by my right hand,
I will lead you to the heights of heaven,
There shall I show you the everlasting Father."
He it is who made the heaven and the earth,
and formed humanity in the beginning,
who was proclaimed through the law and the prophets,
who took flesh from a virgin,
who was hung on a tree,
who was buried in earth,
who was raised from the dead,
and ascended to the heights of heaven,
who sits at the right hand of the Father,

who has the power to save all things,
through whom the Father acted from the beginning and
   forever.
This is the alpha and omega,
this is the beginning and the incomprehensible end.
This is the Christ,
this is the King,
this is Jesus,
this is the commander,
this is the Lord,
this is he who rose from the dead,
this is he who sits at the right hand of the father,
he bears the father and is borne by him.
To him be the glory and the might forever.
Amen.

The Prayer

Father, I want to be a person who says such things. He is risen! And he is risen in me! Come, Holy Spirit, and train me to be such a person of faith. I pray in Jesus' name, amen.

The Question

·   What are your takeaways from this book?

Titles in the Seedbed Daily Text series: